A Cry For Help

Divinely Appointed To Be True to Go Thru

A Cry For Help

Divinely Appointed To Be True to Go Thru

Helen Washington

Anointed Fire™ House Christian Publishing

Copyright Notice
2016
A Cry for Help
Divinely Appointed to be True to Go Thru
© 2016, Helen Washington
(jnhwashington@gmail.com)
Edited by: Steve Robinson

ALL RIGHTS RESERVED. This book contains material protected under International and Federal Copyright Laws and Treaties. Any unauthorized reprint or use of this material is prohibited. No part of this book may be reproduced or transmitted in any form or by any means, electronic or mechanical, including photocopying, recording, or by any information storage and retrieval system without express written permission from the author / publisher.

Disclaimer: This book is designed to provide information and motivation to our readers. It is sold with the understanding that the publisher is not engaged to render any type of psychological, legal, or any other kind of professional advice. No warranties or guarantees are expressed or implied by the author, since every man has his own measure of faith. The individual author(s) shall not be liable for any physical, psychological, emotional, financial, or commercial damages, including; but not limited to, special, incidental, consequential or other damages. Our views and rights are the same: You are responsible for your own choices, actions, and results.

ISBN-13: 978-0998250717
ISBN-10: 0998250716
All scriptural verses were taken from the NIV Bible unless otherwise noted.

Table of Contents

FOREWORD..VII

CHAPTER 1..

In the Beginning.....................................1

CHAPTER 2..

A New Land..15

CHAPTER 3..

I Remember..25

CHAPTER 4..

Eyes of Destruction.............................43

CHAPTER 5..

Into the Wilderness.............................59

CHAPTER 6..

Being Drawn in Darkness...................75

CHAPTER 7..

How A New Life Can Begin...............89

CHAPTER 8..

Caught Up in a Trap.........................103

CHAPTER 9..

Spiraling Self Destruction.................................121

CHAPTER 10..

Hot Pants...129

CHAPTER 11..

A Cry from the Heart...145

CHAPTER 12..

Emptied to be Used for God's Glory..................171

CHAPTER 13..

I Changed Dance Partners..................................191

CHAPTER 14..

The Great Recovery...209

Foreword

Into every life there will be dark days as well as bright ones. We all know that there is no guarantee to how long the light and the darkness will last in our lives. Unfortunately many precious people spend considerable time living their lives in the hopeless darkness of night when they should be living in the glorious and victorious light of day.

In this book there is a very clear and present understanding that a life lived in darkness does not have to end in the darkness of death and hopelessness. The reality of the existence and of the power of God is truly seen throughout the pages of this book. His very power is apparent in its steady thread that flows in love and grace that preserves and directs the lives of those, whom the Lord has chosen unto himself.

This book will bring tears not only to your eyes but also to your very heart. You will find that God has a plan for all of our lives, and He will not give up on those whom He has selected and appointed to know his unexplainable love and compassion. To say that it is God's will for anyone to go through what Mrs. Howard has is not His way nor is it His character for evil to be given as a destiny. But it is his will to show everyone his ability to take what looks to be without hope or a future and turn it around for the good that it was intended. And so it was with the life of Mrs. Howard.

It has truly been an honor to write the forward for this precious woman of God. She has lived through and had to endure such a dark and destructive past.

To have had the joy of being Mrs. Howard's pastor for more than 25 years of her life's journey I can truly say that God's hand has truly been on and in her life. But to God be all of the glory. Only He and He alone could have guided and directed the events of Mrs.

Howard's life so that they would not inevitably destroy her. Seeing the hand of God being present to keep and to sustain her throughout what should have been some life ending times of her life has been truly amazing.

In this book you will see a little girl desiring to be loved and cared for only to be abused and neglected throughout most of her child and adult years. The restoring power of a loving Heavenly Father would become the very reason she is alive to write this book today.

My prayer is for those of you who read this book that you would discover the love and affirmation of the only love that matters, and that is the Lord's love. May you become a witness to the life changing power of God to change any life. No matter the condition that your life may be in He can and He is able to do what no one else can, and that is give you the very life you are intended to live.

D.C. Atkinson Sr. Senior Pastor of the New Bethany Family Worship Center For all Nations.

CHAPTER 1

IN THE BEGINNING

Jesus asked the boy's father, "how long has he been like this?"
"From childhood," he answered.
Mark 9:21

In the Beginning

Everything has a beginning. Everything has a start. Take for instance the caterpillar. Its life begins as a simple egg. There is no great fanfare for an egg. There are no parties thrown for an egg. There are no speeches, dedications, moments of silence or solemn ceremonies conducted for an egg. It's just an egg. But then something amazing begins to happen within that egg, away from nosy human eyes. Its job, its destiny, has been pre-programmed, and the instructions placed deep within its DNA tell it to transform into something else. It can't stay an egg or surely it would die. It has to become a larva, or in plain English, a caterpillar.

While it is a caterpillar it crawls around on its multitude of miniature legs and voraciously devours any leaf from a tree or a plant that has a flower on it. In this stage of rapid development a caterpillar can destroy an entire garden, crop and ecosystem. It's amazing how something so small can wreak so much havoc with potentially long lasting and damaging results. Fortunately it only does this for two weeks before it goes through its next fascinating and equally wondrous stage of development: becoming a butterfly.

What's most incredible about the life cycle of a caterpillar is that in every stage of its development it bears absolutely no resemblance to the previous stage it was in. An egg does not look like a caterpillar, which does not look like a butterfly. All separate and uniquely distinct, yet still all connected.

My life, too, began like this.

The humble state of affairs that framed my beginnings was the dirt road of a sleepy Louisiana town in the home of my great-grandmother, Annie Hart. It was during a time when life for black people, especially in the south, was about one day of prayerful survival after another. Truly no day was promised. It was that bad.

It was right around the turn of the century. Two-thirds of the nation's black population of ten million lived in the rural south. The state of Louisiana was home to some of the most oppressively racist and violent laws that were designed to keep white and black people separate in all areas of life. Jim Crow laws, as they were called (aptly first named after a white man who performed in black face some 70 years earlier in New York) had sprung up throughout the south. These laws were in response, for the most part, to the growing alliances between former black slaves and poor white farmers as they sought to gain control from the exploitation they were being subjected to at the hands of wealthy plantation owners. To an economy that depended on the institution of white privilege, inter-racial alliances had to be crushed at all cost.

My great-grandmother, who was also half Cherokee, worked as a maid. At that time a Black woman was never deemed too much of a threat if she tended to the home of a white woman. In fact, being a maid fit in perfectly with the ideological center of all Jim Crow laws, and that was white supremacy. Whites were to be served by people of color and never the other way around. The life of privilege was supposed to be synonymous with being white. In fact, having a black house keeper in the south was the sign of belonging to a higher class.

Jim Crow laws stipulated that blacks were never to be addressed as an equal, treated as an equal or seen as an equal. Walking on the sidewalk was a privilege reserved for whites only. If a black person ever caught themselves being forced to share the public space of a sidewalk it was their responsibility, including women and children, to walk in the street when a white person walked by.

In the Beginning

This was the time and era of my great-grandmother. The penalty for not acknowledging these laws was prison and death, usually at the hands of an angry lynch mob. These mobs knew that they could act with impunity as no law in the land would disapprove of their deadly acts. It was all in the name of maintaining order and keeping people in line.

This would prove to be very important for one of Annie's children, and helped shape the trajectory of my life.

My great grandmother had 4 daughters and one son whom everyone called brother. She loved them all very deeply, as any mother would. Part of that love manifest itself by her teaching each one of them about the law of the land, namely Jim Crow. It was a reality that every black child growing up at that time had to deal with. There were separate and inferior bathrooms, drinking fountains, and transportation arrangements (to name a few) that became a day to day reality that often needed no explanation. Still, as a loving and nurturing parent, Annie knew that teaching her children how to obey the law was the difference between life and death.

But everyone has their breaking point.

It was on a day that was not unlike any other day. The sun was out, the weather was nice, a cool breeze was blowing through the magnolia trees. Annie understood the predatory nature of many white men who stalked young black women. These men knew that these women had no legal recourse against them and no judge would even entertain listening to them if they ever cried rape or harassment. That's why she always instructed her daughters to accompany one another wherever they went.

It was at a U.S. post office. Her youngest daughter, Catherine, a vibrant, young 16 year old teenager who was probably pregnant at the time with her first child, was standing in line to retrieve a package. More than likely at least one of her other three older sisters was there with her. A white woman, in passing, asked her a direct question. Catherine answered back in a way that the white woman took offense to. (One of the by-products of Jim Crow was that a black person never answer a white person with a tone that could be construed as being stern, smart allicky (uppity) or in any way confrontational.) The fact that this was a very small town where everyone knew each other, this exchange of words grew to include more than just the two of them.

Eventually the white woman found the house where Catherine lived and demanded to speak with her mother. Some time had passed, but the white woman hadn't forgotten the incident. Catherine had grown, and so had her little girl who she had named Verline. By now the year was 1943. At the door this white woman operated with a sense of superiority and supreme right that the prevailing culture of racism inculcated her with. Annie was a total stranger, a grown woman with children and now a grandchild, yet she was reduced to the position of a scolded child, humiliated in front of her own family in her own home. And, as if to add insult to injury, there was nothing she could do about it but to stand there and take it.

"You'd better do something about her before something bad comes this way," the woman shouted. Annie, with her head hung in submission, assured her that it would never happen again.

And she meant exactly what she said. She knew what it meant for word to get around that an "uppity Nigger" lived here. There would be angry mobs of people coming to take Catherine away to teach her a lesson and make an example out of her for anybody else who might think about offending a white woman in

In the Beginning

that way. Those crowds didn't care that Catherine was a young woman herself. Her being a woman meant nothing to them.

There were more lynching murders in the southern states than anywhere else in the country. It has been determined that less than 1% of those lynching murders were as a result of a courtroom conviction. It didn't matter the gender of the person being lynched either. Men, women and children were often lynched in circus style settings after being publicly tortured and humiliated. Sometimes their bodies would be set aflame afterwards and their charred remains left for people to see. It was a horrifically gruesome tool that white supremacists used in order to dissuade any blacks from "getting out of line."

Annie knew that this fate would befall her daughter, so she acted quickly. She did what any loving mother would do. She went to Catherine, and her sisters, and told them that they needed to pack up and leave that night, and not return. That was the only way that she knew of to protect her daughters from the tyranny and horror that would surely be coming their way had the stayed in Louisiana.

Begrudgingly Catherine knew that her mother was right. She had seen the sheer brutality and unrestricted violence that white mobs had been able to get away with. Her community had been affected by laws that provided them with no protection. The daily humiliations that she had to endure were not getting any better, and by now she had a daughter. Who knew when the next white person she speaks to might take "offense" to either what she said or how she said it.

Still, this was home. It was as much her home as it was everyone else's. And that was the bitter pill she had to swallow as she packed up and left that night, leaving her daughter behind with Annie. As a matter of security they were careful not to tell anyone else where she was headed. Only her mother, her sisters and she knew the new destination.

And that destination was a little sleepy desert town called Las Vegas.

CHAPTER 2

A NEW LAND

> *"The Lord appeared to Abram and said,
> To your offspring I will give this land."*
> **Genesis 12:7**

A New Land

The year was 1943, and the social landscape of this small, arid and out of the way city called Las Vegas was beginning to change dramatically.

Named Las Vegas (the meadows) by its former Mexican trade route inhabitants some 100 years earlier, it had become a major stop along the Mormon trail and then further developed by the railroads.

At first it was a dusty outpost of hard scrap workers, farmers and financiers. As it grew so did its reputation of being a place where you could make your own way if you worked hard enough and kept your head down. Its hot, desert location, away from any major source of water and isolated by a rugged range of mountains, attracted a tough, fiercely independent population that didn't mind being self-sufficient and isolated.

A New Land

In 1930 President Herbert Hoover initiated one of the largest and most ambitious public works projects that this country had ever witnessed. It was the construction of the Hoover Dam in Boulder City, which was only 25 miles away. Thousands of men came looking for work and the population quickly grew from 5,000 citizens to over 25,000 people. Construction began right away. The year was 1931.

Along with them came their desires for….companionship and entertainment. But, during this time of prohibition, the federal government quickly outlawed prostitution and gambling in the city of Boulder. So a cottage industry of these "services" grew in the nearby and fully established city of Las Vegas.

As this new industry began to grow, more people came in search of their fortunes. Unfortunately not all of them came seeking to do it legally. Organized crime quickly seized the opportunity to make money in the growing business of legalized gambling and hospitality.

Yet, as the burgeoning city was growing and progressing at breakneck speed, there was one area, in particular, that wasn't progressing at all. In fact, it was quickly sprinting in the opposite direction.

It was the area of race relations.

Blacks moving into Las Vegas weren't welcomed with opened arms. Of the 20,000 workers who worked on the multi-year Hoover Dam project, only 44 were African American. Unions didn't allow them entry. Boulder City, which was federally created and managed was also racially segregated and legally excluded African-Americans from living within its borders. Restrictive housing covenants and prejudicial zoning laws prevented them from moving around freely. By legislative law the west side of town was the only place they were allowed to live. This is the part of town that happened to be the site of a major railroad connection and was characterized by its substandard infrastructure. It truly was "the other side of the tracks".

African-Americans weren't allowed to stay in any of the casinos where they worked exclusively as maids or laborers. They weren't allowed to eat in any of the restaurants that served the hordes of whites who visited or worked nearby. In effect they were pretty much expected to be invisible. And, to make sure they stayed to themselves a very oppressive and reactionary police force had carte blanche to go into their growing communities and commit acts of violence with legal impunity.

In 1941 President Franklin D. Roosevelt issued an Executive Order 8802, effectively prohibiting racial discrimination in federal government and defense industry hiring practices. As a result, the following year Las

A New Land

Vegas began to see a large migration of African Americans from small southern towns.

This was the world that my grandmother Catherine entered when she arrived in 1943.

From a racial standpoint this new place wasn't much different than Lafayette. That didn't slow down my grandmother. She was used to this brand of ignorance. She was looking forward to starting a new life for herself. She had her sisters and she still had a lot of life to live. They had come to live with an aunt, and it wasn't too long before they settled into their new living situation.

Catherine found work as a maid. Back in Louisiana she was hearing that her daughter, Verline, wanted to come and live with her. I imagined that life back there had become too hard for a young, vibrant black woman to endure, especially without her mother.

A New Land

As fate would have it, about two years after my grandmother Catherine moved here, Verline came to be with her and her sisters.

When she finally did make it out to Las Vegas, she hit the ground running. Unlike her mother, Verline loved making friends, especially guys. She was about 16 years old and full of energy, and she didn't have anything, or anyone, holding her down.

Private first class Hampton Gray was a strappingly handsome soldier who her aunts immediately fell in love with. He was stationed at what is now Nellis Air Force Base. When he came knocking Verline didn't even flinch. She liked that he noticed her, but she didn't feel any "magic" between them.

But to her aunts and mother he was like hitting the lottery. A serviceman meant financial security and a way out of the day to day hardships that civilians were forced to endure. But to a young and vibrant Verline, he was just another guy whose attention she enjoyed. The fact that he was in the Army didn't impress her much, but he was crazy about her. So much so that he asked her to marry him right away, because in those days when a man wanted a woman he proposed to her to make her his wife.

Still, she didn't want to disappoint her mother and her aunts, so eventually she relented and said yes. The year was 1946 and she was 16 years old.

They had a son soon after. He doted over Verline and it was evident that he loved and cherished her. Unfortunately she never had the same feelings for him, and as time wore on their marriage began to falter. In six years it was over. He didn't want it to end, but relented when it was evident that the only way that the woman he truly loved would be happy would be if he granted her the divorce she asked him for.

So, with a heavy heart and much to the sadness of her aunts, he granted her wish.

The year was 1952.

Single, and with a son, Verline, who never seemed to have a problem meeting a man, dated quickly. And before you know it, she met a man whom she truly loved. His name was William Hall and two years later in 1954 they got married. She was very happy with William, a man who was also from the south just like her. A few months after they got married she became pregnant with a little girl. That little girl was me, and with her, my older brother and father we would begin our lives together as a family.

The year was 1955.

CHAPTER 3

I Remember

*"For no one is cast off by the Lord forever,
Though he brings grief, he will show
compassion, so great is
His unfailing love."*
Lamentations 3:31

I Remember

When I was a little girl I always loved the holiday season and the joy they would bring. I liked knowing that my family would be together and everybody would be happy as they sat around the table, exchanging stories, laughing out loud and enjoying each other's company. I was at a really cute age, maybe 2 or three if I can remember correctly. My mother used to have me dressed up so cute, like a little doll. I always made sure that I kept my little outfits nice and clean (even at a young age I knew the importance of a matching outfit).

I was a very aware child. There's not much that would happen that I didn't know about. I used to watch everything, from how people interacted with one another to what they were wearing. It's the gift that God gave to me that would serve me well later on in life. Even at a young age I remember being able to tell the seasons by what color the leaves on the trees were. When I saw the color of the leaves begin to change into their rusty, yellow hues it would signal to me that we couldn't stay outside and play as long because the sun set earlier. The desert evenings brought cool, crisp winds that blew away all the dust that had accumulated during the stale hot summer months.

I imagined that our little one bedroom apartment was not unlike many other homes during this time of year. The warm aroma of southern cooking hung high in the air and seemed to coat the upholstery of our modestly furnished home. There was nothing fancy or showy about the furniture. It wasn't cheap looking, but it wasn't exactly new either. It was very practical for the beginning stages of life for the young couple my parents were at the time. I remember helping my mother wash sheets in the bathtub, buff the floors, and clean-up after meals and right before it was time to go to bed.

She worked as a housekeeper for one of the major casinos downtown. I imagined that keeping a clean house became second nature to her after cleaning so many rooms every day. At any rate, ours was a very routine existence, and that worked very well for a precocious little girl like me. In fact, most children thrive in an environment that is structured.

My father worked for Silver State Disposal as a trash collector. Being a trash man was one of the socially acceptable positions that a black man could thrive. Everyone benefitted from them, and because of its more menial and unglamorous job description relegating a black man to "taking out the trash" didn't upset the fragile social pecking order that strict racial segregation sought to uphold.

My dad would often leave home early, especially in the summer months (to beat the heat), and return late, filthy and exhausted. However it was one of the few good paying jobs that were available to him. It was kind of a big deal when he found out he got the job. To have a job in our neighborhood was a big deal, and to have one that paid good and had a good pension? He'd might as well had died and gone to heaven.

Financially, my father always provided for us. Even though he wasn't always back home early, he and my mother did make sure that we always had a roof over our heads and the comforts of a home. My father took great pride in being able to support his family. This was a very important area in his life to him because had he listened to all of the people who knew him as a young boy he would've never thought that he'd experience anything even remotely close to this.

As a young boy he wasn't shown much attention, let alone approval, by his own family. That lack of affirmation left a huge void that, as he got older, he tried to fill by having a family of his own.

But during his youth he was always seeking the approval of others, always trying to show that he mattered. Later in life this would manifest itself as always having to have the best car or the best things or being the best at whatever he did. He needed that kind of recognition to prove to himself that yes, he mattered. Some people would mistake it for pride, when in reality its root was grafted deeply in a childhood hurt and an almost paralyzing insecurity.

His mother, Lucy Bell, had him while she lived in the small village of Epps, Louisiana, located in the extreme northeast West Carroll Parish section of the state. The population there was not unlike most small villages in the south. It consisted mostly of families who had been there for a long time, which meant traditions ran deep. And because it was so remotely located, closer to the western border of Mississippi, the cultural landscape was predictably majority black with a small ruling class of whites.

So, being a young, single black woman with a child in Jim Crow South all but guaranteed that her life would be would be tough. But Lucy was ambitious and decided that the best way to make a better life for her and her son would be to move out west, far away from the humidity and overgrowth of her little sleepy southern alcove.

Leaving baby William behind with her mother, Mattie, she packed her bags and moved to Los Angeles. All of the pictures from there showed people being happy, everyone seemed liked they were doing something. It was so different than Epps and Lucy knew that's where she could start her life anew. It was like a dream world where even the trees looked like long toothpicks with mops for hair.

What made it a little less stressful is that she already had family who had moved there and they told her she could stay with them until she got on her own feet.

That arrangement didn't last very long because soon after arriving she met someone; they fell in love and then got married. Her new name would be Lucy Baker.

With a new husband and a new life she slowly navigated the waters of a very sensitive subject with him; her son back in Louisiana. She knew that it wouldn't be an easy thing to talk about. After all, Mr. Baker had fallen in love with her as a young, single woman and not somebody's mother. So, it was no surprise that when the subject of bringing young William out to Los Angeles to live with them came up, he said "absolutely not." He wasn't fond of the idea of raising another man's child, not to mention that he didn't know the boy.

Back in Louisiana young William was close to 10 years old and full of the type of energy that seems to be only reserved for little boys. I imagined that after having raised her own children the day to day realities of raising a young child was starting to weigh heavily on his maternal grandmother. Eventually she realized that raising a young boy by herself was too much and when she decided it was time for him to go she acted swiftly and without much regard for his well-being. She must've been very tired because, in her haste, she told William that he had to leave. He was only 11 years old, and now he was homeless.

Drifting from one house to another, and sometimes to different family members, young William was eventually taken in by a white family. His time there was spent working for them and in the process he learned how to drive a tractor and do farm work. Feeling safe, he lived with them for a little while until one of his cousins who had already moved to Las Vegas sent for him. He was around 12 years old when he moved to Las Vegas.

I Remember

Having started a new life in sunny Los Angeles away from her son, I'm sure, had started to wear on a newly married Lucy, so she sent for him to come and visit. Over the next several years they tried to reconnect as mother and son and eventually got to a point where they had a good relationship. He visited with her over the summers and they spent a lot of time together.

But Vegas was his home.

When my parents first met my mother had already had a son, Arthur, from a prior marriage. The similarities between my dad's early childhood and that of his new bride's situation were almost identical. But unlike his own mother he did allow Arthur to stay with us from time to time. When he wasn't with us he was with his dad or his father's family.

When I came along I was my mother's first daughter. My grandmother Catherine doted on me. My father was very proud that he had his first child, a little girl. Now there were two children in the house, my brother and I. Our little home was becoming full of the type of newness and life that only young children can bring. Everyone came over to see me, the new baby. My mother's aunts all showed up and took turns holding me while my grandmother sat and watched. We were the perfect portrait of a young, happy family. Everything should've been great except for one unpleasant reality; my parent's marriage was already starting to show signs of strain.

My father's demons of needing the constant approval of those around him began to take a toll on the fledgling relationship that he and my mother had. It had been a few years since they had been married and there were already two children. The psychological warfare of living in a heavily segregated society that everyday provided a whole new level of humiliation and despair had begun to take a toll on them, as it did many black relationships. Let it be told, living under enforced segregation is an emotional and psychological hell for those who had to endure it. By themselves these negative outside forces would've been bad enough.

But then there was the alcohol, which proved to be an accelerant on an already volatile situation.

Both of my parents were drinkers, at times heavy. My father drank prior to getting home from work. As I got older I remember on many occasions him coming home flat out drunk. My mother, on the other hand, would mostly drink with some of her friends once she got home. She'd invite them over and they'd sit around drinking like they were sophisticated socialites. In reality they were mostly a bunch of hardworking women who were in relationships or situations that they would've much rather forgotten about. I don't ever remember alcohol lasting very long in our home.

As the problems in their relationship began to grow our home started to become a less happy place. It became a place that was always tense and sad. My father began to demand that at dinner time he be fed first. We were allowed to eat afterwards. I remember one time my mother prepared something special for him, but he didn't like it so he threw the plate against the wall and watched it shatter into a thousand pieces, food flying everywhere. My mother had to clean it up.

As children we were afraid of my father by now. We never knew when his next outburst would be or what he was capable of doing. It always seemed to center around how he felt he was being disrespected and not valued. My mother was often the object of his most abusive language and I remember their time together seemed to be dominated by their constant fighting. Watching him become incensed over a meal not being prepared right put the whole house on edge. His moods became less and less predictable until one day they culminated into something that a little girl should never see her father doing; hit her mother.

My memories of the event are still painfully vivid. By now my mother had my little sister who was still in her baby chair and couldn't have been more than several months old. I was only 3 years old. My parents were fighting and there was screaming. My sister was crying and I was standing there watching them get louder and louder. I guess my mother had reached a point where she was determined to make a stand because this time she was not backing down from him. This seemed to enrage him even more and as a result he began to raise his hand like he was about to hit her. As his anger increased so did my mother's resolve to not back down.

That's when he hit her in the face. I wanted to run and hide but fear had frozen my legs in place. Then he hit her again, and again. His fists were flying like a piece of paper in a windstorm. My mother tried to back up and protect herself, but he had caught her off-guard with his aggression and temporarily dazed her.

"Stop hitting my mommy," yelled the voice in my head. I was so angry at him. Daddies are supposed to love mommies. They are not supposed to hit mommies. I didn't know what to do. I was helpless to help my mother and that made me angrier at him.

The chaos continued. Blow after blow, my mother was doing her best to deflect his large angry fist from doing more damage. Her children were watching her get beat up. It had to be humiliating beyond words to her. How could she convince her children that she could protect them if she couldn't even protect herself?

I Remember

My sister was in her baby chair screaming and crying hysterically. I imagined that the loud noises frightened her. Later I read that humans are born with an innate fear of loud noises. I can only imagine her anguish, a little baby watching something happen that instinctively she knew was wrong. I didn't know how to react. I was so afraid. There was screaming and hollering and I was experiencing a bunch of emotions that a 3 year old isn't equipped to handle.

My father, in that moment, looked like a wild, crazed animal that had completely lost control, flailing his hands and his fists wildly, striking my defenseless mother about her head and her body with a blind fury. I didn't recognize him anymore and I never looked at him the same way afterwards.

What seemed to last forever was, in reality, only a few seconds. When he figured that he had given my mother the message that her place was not to question anything that he said or did, he stopped. But it wouldn't be the only beating. There would be more. She always healed physically, but the emotional scars ran deep and never went away.

I always blamed my father for what he did to my mother and in turn did to us. He robbed me of a healthy image of how men are supposed to interact with their families. Later in my life I'd realize how much damage this actually caused. But, at that moment, the seed of anger had been firmly planted within me. I hated my father for what he did. Unfortunately, which is often the case with many abused women, the abuse that she suffered became the same abuse that she administered to me, her eldest daughter.

Indeed my life in the lion's den had just begun.

CHAPTER 4

Eyes of Destruction

"The eyes of the Lord are on the righteous, and his ears are attentive to their cry;"
Psalm 34:15

As the size of our family began to grow we eventually moved to a slightly larger, two bedroom apartment. We desperately needed the space as several other babies were soon added to our ranks. And, as you can imagine, with several small children in one house there was a lot of activity going on all the time.

We moved not too far from where we lived before. During those times restrictive housing covenants and zoning laws kept most, if not all black families, regardless of how little or how much they made, in the same general area. So when we moved it wasn't like much really changed.

Likewise the relationship between my mother and father mirrored the same status quo as our living situation. Nothing between them changed either. In fact it seemed to get worse. The fights between them became more frequent, and as a result the general atmosphere of our home became less and less stable. I didn't realize it at the time, but my idea of what a peaceful home meant was being supplanted by all of the violence and confusion I was being exposed to during those young, formative years. This would prove to be disastrous for me as I got older because I never had a standard of emotional stability to use as a point of reference when forming my own relationships.

There was the time that I distinctly remember as a child playing in the grape vines of my great aunt's house and I could hear them fighting inside of her house. Everywhere we went it seemed now like they were always fighting. I never saw them share a tender moment together. I never saw my father express anything but disdain for my mother. Fighting was the dominant activity that I witnessed between them. And now, because they didn't seem to care that others knew (as evidenced by their fight in my great aunt's kitchen) everyone knew what I imagined my mother was trying to keep secret for so long; that she was being abused.

The boldness of my father's physical abuse didn't seem to be met with much surprise or action. During these Ozzie and Harriet days (Ozzie and Harriet was a television show of an ideal American family that expressed the quintessential ideals of the 1950's. The mother and father had two sons, never left home and always worked as a loving team) the ugly reality for women in abusive relationships was quite different. If the police agreed, that's right, agreed to get involved, at worst the abusive spouse was charged with a civil offense. It wasn't until the 80's and 90's that domestic abuse was upgraded to a criminal act, punishable by statutory prison sentences and mandatory restitution. Society's opinion on this heinous crime have changed for the better, but still it is hard to determine the actual amount of cases of domestic violence and women and children who are living under the threat of violence because a lot of women simply don't report it.

In regards to my mother I don't know if she ever contacted law enforcement (who had, at best, a dismissive relationship with domestic abuse victims, especially in the black community) but I do remember there was the occasional visit by child protective services and one time they took away two of my siblings. On occasion, I guess when my mother had enough, we would leave and go to stay with one of my aunts, only to eventually return home after I'm sure that my father begged for forgiveness and asked her to come back. Being a very proud man, losing his family would not have fit into the neat little image I'm sure he had convinced others of. It was like clockwork though, once we returned home the abuse would eventually resume and everything would go back to the way it was.

It was now that I began to notice a change in my mother's overall behavior. There was only so much abuse that she could take and internalize before it had an effect on her personality. I noticed that she began to drink more. She was always tired and depressed. To say that she wasn't happy would've been an understatement. And who could blame her. She had a two-bedroom apartment full of babies all needing her attention, a physically abusive and emotionally absent husband, extended family who knew that she was being abused and a life that seemed to be going in the wrong direction.

Her only solace became the bottle.

When my mother drank it was like she started to overlook things that an attentive mother would pay attention to. For instance, even though our clothes were always clean they began to look tattered and uncared for. Sometimes our hair would get done, and at other times it wouldn't. It all depended on whether or not my father had said or done something that made her mad.

But then something else started happening that I didn't understand at all, nor did I anticipate; my mother began to verbally abuse me. As strange as it sounds I would've expected it from my father. It's what I had become used to after hearing all of the fights between them.

My father was mostly absent, oblivious to my day to day activities. But my mother, the one who I felt a solidarity with, the one who I wanted to protect from my father, the one who I looked to for protection and love began to verbally abuse me, and to a child who was already feeling isolated, confused and angry, this was catastrophic.

I knew that it didn't have to be this way between a mother and a daughter. My father's mother, Lucy, was like a fairy godmother to us. She treated us like little princesses when she saw us. Whenever she visited with us or we went to visit her she showed us the love and attention that a doting grandmother reserved only for her grandchildren. She bought us the cutest clothes, she took us shopping for our mother, and she bought us the nicest most thoughtful gifts and always told us how much she loved us. To a little girl like me it was so important just knowing that someone thought I was special and that I mattered. My grandmother provided that to us, so I knew that it could be done.

But whenever she left, any acts of love and tenderness left with her. I was cast back into the physically threatening and emotionally damaging void of my house. The only thing I learned how to do there was protect myself, and neither my father nor mother made that an easy thing to do.

I never understood why she would turn on me the way that she did. I was simply a little girl with big eyes and a loving heart. All I wanted in return was what any child would've wanted, and that was to feel protected and to be loved. I had watched her take some pretty awful beatings at the hands of my father and did anything I could to comfort her. It was the only thing I could do.

During those awful beatings, she would only shield herself and us. I never saw her try to hit him back. I guess that she had been beat so often that she took on the nature of an abused animal; she figured that fighting back would only prolong the inevitable, so she just laid there and took it.

However there was one time that wasn't the case.

I remember it being really bad on that day. It was late that evening when the hospital released her after receiving treatment for one of the beatings my dad gave her. She took my sister Lizzy and I along with her. When it was time to leave my father didn't come to pick us up. We made our way over to an apartment that I didn't recognize. I had never been there before, but my mother seemed to know exactly where she was going. Storming right up to a door she began banging on it very hard, like she was angry. A woman opened the door and my father wasn't too far behind. My mother pushed her way in and started fighting both of them in front of me and my sister.

I was too young to understand what was going on except that my mother obviously didn't like this woman who she was beating up nor did she like my father for being there. Later I found out that it was merely one of the many women my father had been having an affair with. He had women all over town and apparently my mother knew about them, but never said anything. I imagine that being stranded at the hospital with her two daughters was the straw that broke the camel's back.

In the book of Exodus 34:7 it says that the "Lord maintain(s) love to thousands, and forgiving wickedness, rebellion and sin. Yet he does not leave the guilty unpunished; he punishes the children and their children for the sin of the parents to the third and fourth generation." Later on I learned that my mother's father had pretty much done the same thing with my grandmother. His name was Billy Bob Conwell and he was a very successful and wealthy businessman back in Louisiana. He had 32 children by different women, and because it was such a small and insulated community everyone knew about it. He never married my grandmother and went on to have relationships with a multitude of other women. To add insult to injury he maintained contact and cultivated relationships with many of his other children, but not with my mother.

Now the same fate was beginning to happen to my mother. She had already had several children for a man who was very comfortable with beating her. She had endured pain, humiliation and suffering in front of her children all on account of him. What her father had done to her mother was now happening to her. Maybe this was normative behavior by a man, especially a successful man. Maybe that's why she didn't fight back for so many years because somewhere, deep down, she felt she was no different than her own mother. As a child there was no way that I could process all of this information, none of which I was privy to until I became an adult and started asking questions.

So after feeling caged up like an animal a very natural change started to happen in me. I started to harbor a great deal of resentment towards both of my parents. In reality it was resentment combined with a heavy dose of fear. The inside of my closet started to become my desired location of choice. In there I felt safe, shielded from the chaos that had unfortunately become my daily reality. My closet was quiet and dark. It was the only place I could think and have any peace of mind. I imagine that Jonah must've felt the same way when he was in the belly of the big fish. Had God called me to go to Nineveh I would've said "Nineveh? How about the apartment next door? Anywhere has to be better than this place!"

I began to internalize the awful things my mother would say to me. It was more often than not that she would call me an awful name or put me down. It's as if she needed to elevate herself above the dungeon-like fortress my father's physical and psychological abuse had sentenced her to. And as poorly as she handled the abuse, now she willfully began to heap all of her scorn onto me, a 6 year-old child. There was absolutely no way that I could have processed all of those misplaced, twisted and often alcohol fueled adult emotions.

It became a burden that I wasn't able to bear. So I did what any 6 year old would do under those circumstances: I began to mirror the world that was being forced upon me.

It is said that it only takes three days for a domesticated dog to be left alone, unfed and unloved, before it becomes feral, or goes back to its natural wild state. Once it does this, training it to become the docile, well trained and well behaved furry companion that you've grown to love is next to impossible.

I was becoming that wild dog.

Anger became my dominant characteristic. I was always mad and ready to fight. When I was at school I wasn't one of the good kids. Other kids would pick on me because of the condition of my clothes, and all of the anger that I couldn't address at home found its way to the classroom or the schoolyard.

At home when my mother was abusive to me I didn't have recourse against it. I couldn't hit her back or say anything in response. But while I was at school there was no way that I was going to take anyone's abuse. I was always ready to fight. My anger would send me into blind fits of rage if another kid so much as looked at me in a way that I felt was disrespectful.

I was completely unaware that I had become a great student of what I had witnessed in my own home. My parents never understood the damage that they had done to me, and neither had I. I was empty on the inside and desperately looking for the love that only my grandmothers showed me whenever they could.

I was only six years old, confused, angry and sad. My home life was chaotic and the isolation was almost unbearable. I didn't think that it could get any worse.

CHAPTER 5

INTO THE WILDERNESS

"They did not ask, 'Where is the Lord, who brought us up out of Egypt and led us through the barren wilderness, through a land of deserts and ravines, a land of drought and utter darkness, a land where no one travels and no one lives?'
Jeremiah 2:6

When a ship is at sea and the night stretches its ominous hand of darkness across the sunlit sky the only thing guiding it towards its safe harbor is a lighthouse. This visual life preserver, by way of its outstretched revolving beam of salvation allows the weary captain to know where to steer his vessel through the thick fog and violent storms that make navigation very difficult. It is the sensory troubadour of hope for the people aboard and the families who anxiously await their arrival.

It is no wonder that a singular beam of light from a lighthouse can be the life preserver for something as large as a ship. They have often been compared to angels.

I had two angels in my life when I was younger. They were both like lighthouses that illuminated the rocky shores of the otherwise dark and violent seas that consumed the space around me. I could always count on them to be the safe harbor that a child my age needed and thrived in.

Ironically both of those angels were by maternal and paternal grandmothers.

When I was first born both of them showed me a lot of love and attention. In fact it was during the summer of 1957, when I was almost 2 years old, that I learned to walk. What made it so memorable is that my parents and I were at Lucy's house in Los Angeles when it happened. Even as a baby I seemed to thrive under her care and attention.

The love that I received from her was unconditional. Whenever she came to visit with us in Las Vegas she'd take us shopping and buy us (my younger sister and I) the cutest dresses and outfits. I remember her always being mindful of our mother as well, and she would illustrate that by allowing us to pick out nice clothes for her too.

We were always very excited to know when she was coming to visit or when we would be going to visit her. Her husband, I remember, was a very kind man who allowed her to spoil us and spend as much time with us as she wanted. She doted on us.

Lucy was a very important person in my young life because it was through her that I knew there was a better way for people to treat one another. All I had been constantly exposed to at that point was the pervasive and psychotic dysfunction of my parent's house. Lucy provided comfort and warmth that, while it was foreign to us, seemed to feel, I don't know, natural.

Whenever she came around there was calm. Whenever she was there we seemed to forget about our struggles. Even though my father was able to provide for us financially, having a lot of kids coupled with the drinking and other women in his life, we lived in what could best be described as functional poverty. Living in an apartment complex with other families who lived like we did provided for a very chaotic and busy existence.

In other words misery loves company. People of like means tend to want to live around other people of like means. It's somewhat of a social security blanket to know that your neighbor isn't doing that much better than you're doing. If I had a tough day it isn't so bad to know that, most likely, they had a tough day also. At our table there were a bunch of mouths to feed and likewise they had a bunch of mouths to feed as well. In other words, their struggles were our struggles. Everyone knew each other, maybe too well.

When Lucy was around us there came with her a calm serenity. It seemed to flower around her and flow through her. Everyone felt it. She was a special woman who seemed to have a genuinely kind word for everyone she came in contact with. They were all touched by her warmth and sincerity.

I'm sure she knew about the wretched condition of my parent's marriage. Looking back on things with an adult's sensitivity I'm convinced that's why she insisted on staying nearby at one of her sisters or brothers homes. We loved going over there as children. It was like a vacation being able to stay somewhere that wasn't our crowded home. Plus the evidence of abuse was everywhere. There was no denying that. In spite of it all she took her assignment of sharing the love of Christ with her grandchildren very seriously and with loving kindness.

There was nothing else in my life at that time that even remotely resembled the beauty that she brought with her when she came around. Even though my great aunts claimed to be Christian you would never know it by the fruit that fell from their trees. In fact I only remember going to church on maybe Easter and Mother's day. Other than that it was hell as usual.

That wasn't the case with Lucy. She truly lived the word of God through her every action. She knew that we didn't have a lot of extra money. She never imposed on my parents or tried to involve herself in the messy dynamics of their relationship. Rather she chose to be a gentle and very wise guiding light for her grandchildren.

She introduced us to memory scripture verses and church hymns. She loved singing them along with us and even bought my family an organ so that we could play the songs how they were sung in church. Her love for us was undeniable and we always hated to see her have to go back to Los Angeles.

After her husband died she got remarried. This was later on in life. After that we didn't see much of her anymore. But she had already planted some powerful seeds within us that would blossom much later in life.

My maternal grandmother was literally the rock that kept my family together. She too extended her undying love and support to me and my siblings in the midst of our family turmoil. When my mother would gather up enough courage to leave my father it was to my grandmother's house that we would always retreat. No matter how many of us were coming over she would always have enough food prepared for us to eat and safe, warm arms for us to be sheltered by.

Everyone loved her. I was so proud to share her name. I wanted to be just like her. I remember one time when I was a little girl and she and I went shopping together and I fell in love with a dress that she was going to buy for herself. She found one in my size and wound up getting it for me instead. I felt so loved by her, and for a little girl with my home life I literally clung onto the way she loved and adored me. I needed someone to tell me I was okay and that I mattered. My mother's mother did that. I often wondered why and how my mother turned out the way she did, and it wasn't until years later that I was able to reconcile how she could be so different from her own mother.

But as a child I didn't even consider that. All I knew was that grandmama loved me, people loved her and I had her name, which meant people should've loved me like they loved her. That's at least the way my mind worked when I was a child.

Our bond was inseparable. Everywhere she went, I went. The people she knew all knew of me, her little grandbaby. I never felt anything but love from her.

One day my sister and I were playing in our house and my grandmother sat down on the couch to rest. She was beginning to get older and couldn't stay on her feet as long as she would like. She had always been a very active woman and didn't like staying idle for too long. Her southern work ethic was a very hard habit to break. She was always cleaning something or moving things around. It was just how she was. But today she was tired and it was around noon, plus her two grand-daughters were playing in the house. Surely they'd be able to wake her up should something happen. Plus my mother was there.

Within a few minutes of her going to sleep on the couch my younger sister said "mama, what's all that white stuff comin' out of grandmother's mouth?" My mother went and checked on her, but she wouldn't wake up. She frantically ran outside to the neighbor's house across the yard and begged them to call the ambulance because something was wrong. People started panicking. My father had gone to the liquor store and someone ran over there to go and get him.

By the time he made it back home the ambulance had already arrived and everyone in the neighborhood was standing outside looking. Everyone who knew my grandmother loved her. Her sister's had all come by as well to check and see what all the commotion was. When they saw the ambulance they panicked and rushed the house, only to be restrained by the police.

I was so afraid because I had never seen my grandmother like that before. She had just sat down to take a nap on her couch like she had many times before. As a matter of fact it was routine to walk in and see her asleep on the couch. This was nothing new. But what was new was the fact that there she was, slumped to the side with all of this stuff that looked like white foam oozing from her mouth.

The image still haunts me to this day.

Into the Wilderness

When the fire department and the ambulance arrived they put everyone out of the house and immediately began working on my grandmother, who was not waking up.

By now a crowd had begun to grow outside as people were all getting news that my grandmother was ill and the police and fire department were all in our house. We all stood outside waiting to get word from any of the people who were working to revive her. We wanted to know that she was going to be okay.

It was very stressful. People were crying and holding onto each other, hoping that there was going to be good news.

And then that's when the front door to our house opened and a few of the emergency workers walked out. Behind them were two men carrying a black body bag with the remains of my grandmother. What had been optimistic anxiety immediately turned into heart wrenching grief. People began screaming because they couldn't believe that she was dead. My mother was inconsolable at the sight of her mother in a body bag. Couldn't they have just put her in the ambulance before they put her in a body bag?

I couldn't believe it. I cried uncontrollably because I had just seen her a few minutes earlier. She was just tired and had taken a short nap, like she had done many times before, and now she's gone? My little mind couldn't even digest all of the ingredients that surrounded what had just happened. I'm sure that I was in shock. I simply didn't know how to handle the fact that the woman who was my protector, my sometimes care giver and my grandmother was now gone. It didn't seem real to me.

Later we found out that she died from a massive heart attack while she was sleeping. She never experienced any pain. The doctors said that she went quickly and quietly and that even if she had been in a hospital that the chances of saving her were slim to none.

Her death put me in an all-out panic. Who was going to love me now? No one at home did. Who's going to protect me now? No one at home did. Who's going to teach me now? No one at home did. Who's going to hug me and tell me "baby, it's gonna be alright?"

The fact that she had several other sisters was lost on us. None of them were going to "step up" and be like a grandmother to me. In fact they, along with their children, had pretty much shunned us, primarily because of my father and the way he treated my mother.

With my grandmother being gone I had nowhere to run and nowhere to hide. I sank into a deep depression knowing that my most difficult days would probably be ahead of me.

Little did I know that, upon her death, my life would never be the same.

She died in 1967. I was only 11 years old. On the day she was buried I cried tears of sadness for her, and also for me. I didn't know what was about to happen to me. I was completely lost. I thought I had hit bottom.

Now that my two lighthouses had been extinguished, who would be there to guide me away from the rocky sea shores that would surely be my ruin? The ocean currents of my life were starting to overtake me and now I had nowhere to turn for help. I was a scared, lonely, angry and a depressed little girl.

CHAPTER 6

Being Drawn in Darkness

"Even though I walk through the darkest valley, I will fear no evil, for you are with me; your rod and your staff, they comfort me."
Psalm 23:4

The day wasn't unlike any of the other days. The sun was high in the sky, like a bright lantern set high on a tree branch. The winds had whipped up a healthy cloud of dust and it was hot. In other words it was just another summer day in Las Vegas.

I think it was around summer break because I don't remember being in school at all. We always got out before the summer heat got out of control, so it must've been around the middle of May.

The apartment complex where we lived was full of families that had little children running around which made it a very fun and noisy place. I remember that we always had other kids our age to run around and play with. Even though my home life was tumultuous at best, on those few occasions where I got to run around and be a kid, laughing and screaming, it actually felt nice. Plus we had cousins who lived in the next complex over from us and they were still allowed to come and play with us during the weekdays (this would change as we got older).

When we were out of school our days were filled with the routine that poverty inflicted on us. Finding things to do required an active imagination, something that I don't see in many children today. There were no video games back then. Sometimes an empty can or an empty box became our gateway to hours of gleeful enjoyment. The simplest distractions turned into the focus of hours of entertainment.

As I was running around and playing with some of my other little friends I somehow wound up inside one of their apartments. Our building wasn't that big so I wasn't too far from our unit. My mother hadn't left for work yet and was still at home with some of my younger siblings. Even though there was no adult supervision I still felt safe knowing my mother was still so close by.

While in the apartment we continued to play and have the type of innocent fun that most 11-year-olds would. I don't recall exactly what we were doing but it wasn't anything that would get us into trouble. The last thing I wanted to do was to do something that would make my mother even angrier than she already was. Giving her another reason to yell at me was not high on my list of things to do. As it was she didn't seem to need much of any reason outside of the fact that I was simply there breathing the same air that she did.

Distracted by our running around and playing I didn't notice two older boys when they walked in. I don't know if they both lived there or not. I kinda recognized one of them, but the other one I hadn't seen before. They were probably around 16 or 17. I don't remember except for the fact that they were so much bigger than we were. It didn't matter though. I was only 11. Their world and ours never intersected. Plus I was so full of anger and bitterness that the fact that two older guys were now in the house made me tense, which I later recognized as being the only reaction I was programmed to have thanks to the way my father treated my mother and the rest of us.

Apparently they convinced us to come to one of the back bedrooms. At first I hesitated knowing that I would probably get in trouble if my mother found out. But, again, I was so angry that I quickly overcame my hesitation and joined the rest of my friends, and the two older boys in the back room. We were young and innocent and quickly fell under their influence as little kids looking for something to do often will.

After a series of events, somehow I wound up being left alone in the room with these two teenage boys. One of them approached me from behind and grabbed me. Immediately I went into complete fear mode, which made me lash out at them. I was starting to go into the first stage of panic. I knew that I shouldn't have been there. What would my mother think if she saw me in the room with these boys?

I wasn't afraid of fighting. I had seen it in my house from the time I was a little girl. I knew how to hit somebody in a way that it would hurt them. I had already been in more fights than I could remember at school. People who knew me knew that I wasn't afraid to throw down.

But there is no amount of lashing out or fighting that a 11 year old can do to ward off the strength of a 16 year-old assailant. I felt one of them place their entire weight on top of me, holding me down. I was on my stomach and he had pressed down on my back so that I could barely breathe, let alone move. I didn't know what was happening but I was frozen with fear and tried to squirm my way out of whatever it was they had planned for me. I started kicking violently to free myself, but the other one restrained my legs.

No amount of fighting I did prevailed. I felt one reaching for my panties and instantly knew that something bad was about to happen. My eyes filled with tears and my breathing became more erratic. I was so scared and so angry. I couldn't even scream.

As the other boy held me down, on that typically hot routine summer day in Las Vegas, Nevada I had my 11-year-old body violated in the ugliest and vilest manner.

Right then and there, against my will, I reluctantly renewed my membership in the sorority of sexually assaulted women.

Nationally 1 out of every 6 American women have been victimized by this horrendous act of violence. Rape doesn't care how old you are, it doesn't care where you went to school and it doesn't care what you do. It doesn't care if you live in the ghetto or in a penthouse suite. Rape is the ultimate act of violence against a woman of any age. Juvenile rape often goes unreported due to the stigma that it can leave on a young woman. In most cases of juvenile sexual assaults the victims know their attacker.

Statistically, rape is often committed between people who know one another, the most common occurrence happening between family members. In this instance I didn't know my attacker, but, sadly, like so many other young women this was not the first time I had been abused. It had happened several years earlier, when I was only 4 or 5. That time it did happen in my own home.

My parents were having one of their get-togethers where their friends and family (mostly friends) came over to drink, play cards and have a good time. There was no special occasion that they were celebrating. It was just an excuse to come by our house, get drunk and then go back home. They had them all of the time, so it wasn't out of the ordinary for me to be around a lot of older people.

I remember having to go to the bathroom and when I turned around there was a man standing behind me. I don't remember if he was a family member or not. In fact I tried to block out as many of the memories as I could, which is a typical coping mechanism of most children who have been sexually victimized.

I do remember that he put his hands down my pants and fondled me. I was only 4 or 5 years old at the time. I had no idea what was going on, but I did know that it was wrong. That event only fueled the anger that I had growing inside of me. I never told anyone because I was afraid and ashamed. How does a child that young process something like that, especially when they haven't been experiencing any of the love and affection that would let her know that she would be supported and not blamed?

Now, again, here I was, 11 years old, and my body and soul were both defiled with the filth of a perverted and twisted mind.

Looking back on it, in a lot of ways I was the poster child for something like this happening. I came from a deeply dysfunctional home where my parents had pretty much abandoned me, showing me little or no affection at all. The abuse I had witnessed between my parents had permanently marred my reality of a healthy male/female relationship dynamic. I was completely and utterly lost. My own agony prevented me from seeing the warning signs that led up to the series of events that I was now going to have to live with for the rest of my life.

What little innocence I had was lost.

Being Drawn in Darkness

Even though my mother was home on that day she wasn't looking out for me. In fact, during this time in her life she had started drinking heavily, so her judgment was skewed at best.

And now this happened.

Eventually my assailants let me go after hearing that another adult was entering the apartment. They both quickly slithered away and left me lying there alone. I was completely humiliated as I too left that place of shame and quickly returned to my own apartment room, shunning the attention of any of my childhood friends who, only a few moments earlier, I shared innocence with. Now they seemed so far away from me, so different than where I was. I felt dirty, ashamed and further alienated from anyone else around me.

I convinced myself that, should people find out about what happened, that they would've thought that somehow it was my fault. After all my mother and father didn't like me, I didn't have any friends that I could talk to because I wasn't able to form relationships very well (which I later found out was a symptom of my abuse) and now I had to carry this guilt and shame with me. My grandmother had recently passed away so there was no one to protect me and no one for me to talk to.

It was too much for a 11-year old. I couldn't handle it, so I went to my room and hid in my closet because that had become my happy place, the only place where I felt safe. I hid in my closet and didn't tell a soul what had happened. It wasn't the right thing to do, but it was the only thing I knew how to do.

CHAPTER 7

How A New Life Can Begin

"Before I formed you in the womb I knew you, before you were born I set you apart; I appointed you as a prophet to the nations."
Jeremiah 1:5

How a New Life Can Begin

It can easily be said that my life, up to this point, had been pretty bleak. It's amazing that in such a short amount of time so much hurt and pain could be compiled. By the time I was 10 I had already been a witness to innumerable fights between my parents, an unfulfilling home life, both emotional and sexual abuse and the death of the only person who protected me, my maternal grandmother.

No wonder I was so angry, lonely and confused. No one, let alone an innocent child, should have to learn how to navigate the world that I had to learn to navigate and thrive in. It was a task that, sadly, I didn't think I was prepared to handle.

In a lot of ways my story was a lot like a woman named Ruth. She was a woman in the bible who had a treacherous beginning, but a happy ending. And, during a time when women had it hard, Ruth became the ancestor of Jesus, the messiah. She was even mentioned in the New Testament, one of a very few women from the Old Testament, she was included in Jesus' ancestral blood line in Matthew 1:5.

Most modern day teachers like to focus on the fact that Ruth, in spite of all that she had gone thru, wound up marrying a very wealthy man named Boaz who loved her in spite of her past. Indeed it is a very heartwarming and uplifting story in the bible that resonates well with a modern western society's idea of success.

But let's look at the details of the story a little closer.

Ruth was a Moabite woman who lived amongst the Jews. The Moabites were despised as a people by the Jews because of their lineage, namely because they came from the union of Lot and one of his daughters who deceived him by getting him drunk and sleeping with him.

Additionally, as a people, they were not very hospitable to the Jews during their Exodus from the land of Egypt. On top of that the very proud and arrogant Moabites led Israel into idolatry when their men intermarried with their women.

In other words, there was no love between these two people.

In today's terms imagine that you live next door to a person whose family had been extremely prejudicial and unjust to your family for many, many years. How would you feel about becoming friends with them, especially if they never expressed remorse for having repeatedly done horrible things in the past?

Now you understand the relationship between the Moabites and the children of Israel.

In the book of Leviticus, the God of Abraham laid out all of the laws and regulations that he required of the children of Israel in order for them to be separate and holy. There were many nations surrounding them as they travelled through the desert to the land that God had promised to them. While they travelled they undoubtedly picked up people along the way who were not part of them when they left Egypt. One of the rules that God gave them through Moses was that they treat foreigners who observed and respected their customs with respect.

When famine struck the land of Israel many Jews left in search of food. They often travelled to neighboring nations and took their customs with them. This was the case of a man named Elimelek. He took his wife, Naomi, and two sons with him to Moab, the land of the Moabites.

Famine is never a good thing. When there's not enough food to eat people begin to perish. This is what undoubtedly spurred Elimelek to move his family.

We'll call this strike number one.

During that time a woman was considered to be the property of her husband. Her testimony in a court of law had no standing nor was there any government aid provided for them upon the death of the men who "covered" them while they were married. It is very important to remember that. For a woman, being married meant that she now had legal standing. She was a blip on the radar screen of "yes, we now acknowledge you."

This was the cultural construct of the day and had great significance for the next series of unfortunate events.

The bible doesn't say how, but Elimelek died (strike 2), leaving his wife "uncovered" except for the fact that she had two sons. They provided her legal standing. They were married to Moabite women, one's name was Orpah and the other's name was Ruth.

How a New Life Can Begin

Again something happened and both of Naomi's sons died (strike 3) leaving Naomi with absolutely no male covering, thus no legal standing. She was now officially a widow along with her two daughter-in-laws.

Naomi decided that it would be best if she went back to the land of her people. (I think one of the reasons for this was because, as prescribed in the book of Leviticus 23, there were provisions that were to be made for the poor and the foreigner living among them.) As she left she bid her daughter-in-laws farewell and wished for them to find new husbands (and thus new legal covering).

One daughter-in-law left and went back to what she knew, which was the land of her people. The other daughter-in-law stayed with Naomi and went to a land she didn't know.

Once in Israel Ruth was Naomi's faithful servant and showed deep love towards her. She

How a New Life Can Begin

gained respect in the community because of how well she treated Naomi and how good her character was. Still, Naomi was much older and wiser and wanted her daughter-in-law to be remarried.

During that time people farmed and brought their grains to a community threshing floor. It was there that stories were exchanged and all of the community news was dispersed. Community threshing floors were the property of either one person or the community as a whole.

Boaz was a wealthy older man who had his own threshing floor. Naomi, being wiser and very shrewd, gave Ruth specific instructions (that would be considered scandalous even by today's standards) on how to get Boaz to notice her.

Do you remember how a woman needed a man's "covering" in order to have social standing in the community? There was also another very important issue at play here, and that was the legal reality of tribal land inheritance.

In the book of Numbers God made it very clear to Moses that in order for a tribe to maintain its proportionate amount of land that women had to marry within their clan. If a woman married outside her clan the right that clan had to their proportionate slice of the land pie diminished. Ruth was a Moabite, someone who wasn't beholden to this policy, but because she loved Naomi so much she adhered to this practice of intra-clan marrying.

Boaz was undoubtedly within the same clan as Naomi, but Naomi, being too old to remarry, guided Ruth in the way that she should go. Eventually Boaz married her, further allowing her to gain social standing in a culture that required intra-clan unions and one that didn't see women as being equal to men.

How a New Life Can Begin

Why was Ruth so important? First of all, she came from a despised nation of people who weren't even supposed to inter-marry with the children of Israel. Secondly she lost her husband and came to a foreign land with nothing. Thirdly she had to establish herself among a people who, for the most part, only treated her well because they were told to.

You think she had it tough? Absolutely! But God held her faithfulness to Naomi in such high esteem that he allowed her to become the great-grandmother to David, the king of Israel, and a direct ancestor to Jesus. So while her life started off as being full of great sorrow, the small seed of faith that she had, as displayed in her love shown towards Naomi, a woman she shared no blood bond with, ultimately saved her in the end.

And, like Ruth, I had a small seed planted in me that would not blossom for many

How a New Life Can Begin

years. That seed was planted there by my paternal grandmother, Lucy.

If you asked my family back then if they were Christian they would've all said a resounding "yes!" They were all from the south and all southerners were Sunday only Christians by birth, or at least that's what they were lead to believe. It wasn't until Lucy would come and visit us that we would actually learn what a real Christian was.

She would show us how to pray and learn how to sing bible songs. She was a wonderful woman of God who knew that our home was starved of anything resembling the gospel. So, when she did come to visit us when we were little she would give us bible verses to remember and recite. She even bought my family a church organ so that we could sing the songs the way she liked to hear them sung on Sundays. She always prayed with us and for us while she was around. Her presence was always accompanied by a great sense of warmth and peace that seemed to disappear when she wasn't around.

I never knew it then, but the spiritual seeds she planted in us were hard at work trying to find some good soil to grab ahold of. I believe that's why the enemy came after me so strong, because he knew that once the roots took hold that there would be nothing that would hold me back from proclaiming the word of God to as many people as I could.

But that would be a long way off still. The appointed time that God had given me had not yet arrived. There were still some things that I had to go through.

Like the children of Israel, I was still walking around in the desert. The land of milk and honey lay far off in the distance.

CHAPTER 8
CAUGHT UP IN A TRAP

"Among my people are the wicked who lie in wait like men who snare birds and like those who set traps to catch people."
Jeremiah 5:26

Caught Up in a Trap

Young women in the same circumstances that I encountered while I was growing up hide their pain by acting out in the most outlandish and inappropriate ways. They do this for two reasons: 1) to get attention because they're hurting so bad and they want someone, anyone to love them; 2) the environment they grew up in has stunted their ability to form healthy relationships with others. As a result of wearing these two different faces they often spare no costs in convincing people around them that they're in charge and in control of everything that's going on around them.

But that's just the mask that they wear and it's the act they've perfected. The reality, behind that mask, is quite different. Inside they're dying for guidance and attention, for a loving hand to reach down and correct their self-destructive behavior. I know because I was one of those girls when I was 13.

Caught Up in a Trap

In a lot of ways my parents had become more like detached adult friends who I lived with. They had long ago stopped showing me any kind of attention that you would think they would show to a young, impressionable little girl. By then I had started smoking cigarettes in an effort to be grown. When I ran out all I had to do was ask my father for one of his parliament cigarettes and he would give it to me. There was no regard for my well-being. In their eyes I was pretty much another adult in the house.

I had a job working in one of the hotels as a housekeeper. Because I was still in school I mostly worked on the weekends. Again there was no regard for the type of people I was around or the places I would go. I came and went as I pleased. I was driving. My father taught me how, I guess so that I wouldn't have to bother him to take me places. I was even happier about that. I was basically totally on my own by now.

Caught Up in a Trap

When I was away from home I was able to reinvent myself as a sophisticated, fearless and in charge young woman. I bought my own clothes, I bought my own food, and I had my own separate world away from them. No one knew I was 13 except my family, and they were often nowhere to be found.

I don't know when the disconnect between my parents and I happened, or why. I still think about it to this day, of the actual event that caused us to be the way we were back then. I don't remember any one situation occurring where I broke some long standing rule that put me in their dog house. Rather it was more like a ship that slowly, but over time, drifted further and further out to sea until no one could see it anymore.

They had shown that they were capable of the type of kindness and consideration that loving, caring parents show.

Caught Up in a Trap

When I was younger I accidentally knocked scalding hot water on my arm and left leg and had to go to the hospital for treatment. My entire family, including my mother and father, came to visit with me. I even had one of my favorite teachers from school show up and visit me. When I got home my mother was very attentive to my needs for a few weeks, making sure that I had everything that I needed and that I was comfortable. All of my family came by to visit with me and things at home were pretty good.

But that didn't last long. Eventually things returned back to the icy cold waters of avoidance and neglect that I had become accustomed to. It was okay by then. I had finally arrived at an age where I could fend for myself pretty much all the time if that's what I had to do.

And I was pretty good at it. I was tough, I could defend myself, I had a job, I had my own money, I was dressing myself the way I wanted to look. In my own mind I was "the business".

It's no shock that people would take notice. I was always surprised by their compliments because after all the years of abuse at home I didn't feel like I deserved it. After all when you're mistreated and neglected for so long you start to believe it. So when people are kind you never really believe them. You're constantly trying to figure out what angle they're trying to approach you with. You don't trust people because you don't want to get hurt again. You deny yourself the basic human need of affection and companionship and usually replace it with something far less positive.

This is where the boy entered into my life.

It didn't start off as anything bad. As a matter of fact he did everything in order. He

Caught Up in a Trap

asked my parents if he could be allowed to date me. It was chivalrous to say the least. I imagined that he saw me being quite the independent young woman who dressed very nicely and he wanted to get to know me better. There was nothing wrong with that.

He was kind of a distant family friend. His sister was my mother's best friend. She approached my mother with the request from her brother that he was interested in going out with me. Once again, there was nothing inherently wrong or out of the ordinary about his request.

What was outrageous was that he was 19 years old, and my parents knew that I was only 13. I may not have acted like I was 13, but I was, and they knew it. And, living where we did everyone knew, except me, what was on the mind of a 19-year-old boy. This simple fact should've prompted them to deny his request.

Caught Up in a Trap

But it didn't. They gave their full blessing to us dating.

When I found out that my mother's friend had a brother who was interested in me, in my mind, the mind of a lonely, hurt and angry 13-year-old girl, it must've meant that he really liked me. After all I hadn't known that emotion with any regularity so I quickly became infatuated with the idea of an older boy wanting to pay attention to me.

Our "romance" wasn't much on fanfare. I don't recall ever really going out and doing anything. We were both kids, at least I was. Most of our activities took place either at my house or at someone else's home. Naturally I was very receptive to any and all forms of attention. This was all new to me, the feelings of being in love and having someone to talk to. And even if it meant that he wasn't really listening to me, it didn't matter. All I wanted was someone who showed me attention, and made me feel that I mattered.

And in return for his attention, what was there for me to offer? I was only 13. I had no life experiences that I could share, no point of reference to use as a guidepost for my actions. I wasn't a very good student because of my home life, and I was still a little girl. What on earth could I have in common with a 19 year-old boy, 6 years my senior in age and I don't know how many years older than me in experience.

He never showed signs of being mean to me. He was always nice and made sure to be respectful to my parents. After all it was them who gave him the keys to the kingdom by handing me over to him, so to them he had to show respect and admiration. He really didn't have much of a choice.

And what did we do when we did have moments alone with one another? For a 13-

year-old girl, and for most young attention-starved girls, the ultimate and only redeemable form of gratitude that they can express is with their bodies.

The young men in my neighborhood didn't understand or appreciate any other form of a response to them showing you any attention. It was understood that sex was going to be a part of the relationship. And let me make something very clear, it wasn't as if he forced himself on me when that time came. In my mind, one that had been formed in the chaos of absenteeism and neglect, I felt that it was right.

This boy was going to be my husband. I was going to be his wife and we were going to live happily ever after. He was going to rescue me from my parents and move me into our own apartment. I was going to have his baby and we were going to be one big happy family. I had already planned it out in my head as I lay there with him.

Then reality hit. After all of our raw, unfettered and unprotected passion I found out that I was going to be his baby's mother. Unfortunately I also found out that I wasn't going to be the only woman who would have that title. There were others. Not only did he already have a girlfriend who had a two-year old by him but there was another girl who was 6 months pregnant with his baby while I was 3 months pregnant with his son.

My little neatly put together fantasy had quickly devolved into the fiery depths of being one big hot mess. When I found out the extent of just how messy things were news had already traveled around our very tightly knit neighborhood and one of the other baby's mothers had made up in her mind that she was gonna find me and beat me up. I imagine she didn't care too much for me even though we were both victims of the same guy. If anything she should've been mad at him. But that's not how it happened, so one day when I was walking home, pregnant of course, here she comes jumping out of the bushes trying to ambush me. I was so angry at the time that I got the upper hand on her and whipped her so soundly that she ran away.

Afterwards I decided that I didn't want to have anything else to do with him, and I quickly stopped having any contact with him.

When I became pregnant I was conflicted in my emotions. On one hand I felt that somebody loved me enough to want to be with me. No one had shown me that kind of attention before, and I soaked it up like a sponge.

On the other hand my parents would be infuriated with me. The visual evidence of us having been intimate would drive a wedge even further between us, especially between my mother and I being that this was her best friend's little brother.

How could I be so stupid?

But then, the strangest thing happened to me. It's like someone, or something, stepped inside of my mother and she became this loving, caring creature that I had never seen before. As my pregnancy progressed she actually became, dare I say, a loving, kind, caring and attentive mother. There was no way I could've seen this coming. I had nothing to compare it to.

Maybe I was dreaming.

It was the oddest thing, but I soon became quite spoiled by all of the love she was showing me. I can't say I knew or even slightly recognized this new person. But I can say one thing.

I liked it!

Throughout my entire pregnancy my mother cared for me in a way that I hadn't even known she was capable of. Gone were the arguments, the loud talking and the name calling. It was as if I had landed on a luxury cruise ship with my own balcony, maid service, chef and housekeeper. Every day was a holiday.

I was chillin!

The problem was that my cruise ship had a 9 month expiration sticker on the ticket.

It went like this:

When the day came for me to have my baby my parents were there with me. I didn't know what to expect, and being so young I had absolutely no idea of what was about to happen. All I knew was that I was ready to have this baby and enter into a new, loving relationship with this new woman who I had lived with for the past 9 months who strongly resembled my mother.

After I had gone through what seemed like an eternity of agonizing labor I finally delivered a healthy baby boy. The hospital dressed him in powder blue newborn clothes and handed him to me. I was happy and nervous all at the same time. I didn't know what the future would hold for me, but I did know that I was going to have to make some changes in my life now that I had a precious little baby of my own.

After about a day I got to take him home, a 14-year- old mother. Looking back on it I can only imagine what the nurses must've been saying when they saw me, a child, being wheel-chaired out of the maternity ward and into a waiting car holding a brand new baby.

As soon as my baby boy was born things went right back to the way they had been before I was pregnant. Hello neglect, hello name calling, hello emotional abuse.

My old friends, indeed, were back, and with a vengeance. After I had my son it was like she wanted to make up for lost time. If the abuse was bad before, she doubled down on it once I brought my baby home.

When we got home all of my brothers and sisters came running out to see their new little nephew. I looked at them all, with their wild-eyed innocence still intact, and felt even more estranged from them than I ever had before.

CHAPTER 9

Spiraling Self Destruction

"There is a way that appears to be right, but in the end it leads to death."
Proverbs 16:25

Spiraling Self Destruction

As I got older I often fell into a pre-programmed trap of bad decision making. I'd say that from the age of 12 years-old I was in complete control of the type of decisions that I was going to make. At the age of 13 I knew what was right and what was wrong. There was no excuse for my self-destructive behavior at that point. I knew better and made the wrong decisions.

This was often the most trying time in my life because all of the anger and bitterness that I was feeling towards others had started to eat away at my insides. I didn't like myself nor what I had become, so I continued to do things to myself that distracted me from feeling so empty.

Yes, there were drugs. When I was barely 14 years-old I was introduced to sleeping pills by a woman who was old enough to be my mother. In retrospect she should've been someone who took me under her wing and helped me to lead a better life.

Now that I look back on it I realize that she was very unsettled in her own life and probably identified with the mess that my life had become. In me she saw a younger version of her wretched self. Because of that all she wanted to do was pull me in deeper. Truly misery loves company. It was like I was in a barrel full of crabs, and as soon as I would start to try to crawl out someone would grab me and bring me back down.

She gave me a steady supply of sleeping pills. I was so young and confused that I didn't know any better, so I always took them. She fed them to me like a mother bird feeds its babies.

During those days I don't remember not being high. In fact if I wasn't high something was wrong. My daily life was miserable and all I wanted to do was escape. It was the fact that I had been exposed to the lives and material things of people who had more than I had that made me really start to hate the fact that every day I awoke to a small, crowded apartment with crying babies and fighting parents.

When people are unhappy with their lives drugs provide an escape. This is why so often drug abuse is so closely tied to poverty. A lot of poor people have nowhere to go to get help. Sometimes they have so many problems that it's hard to even know where to begin to try and help. So, what happens many times is that people living in these terrible conditions start to self-medicate. When you're poor the neighborhood pharmacist is the drug dealer.

I'm not saying that only poor people abuse drugs, because that's not true either. What I am saying is that if you're young, poor and living in an abusive environment like I was getting high doesn't seem like such a bad thing.

That's where I was at that point in my life. Being high was a welcome retreat from the nightmare that my life had become. The pills that she gave me kept my mind distracted from my day to day reality. I stayed tuned out as much as possible.

Here's a case in point. After I had my child and I was living back at home (remember, I was still only a child) I overheard my mother talking really bad about me. The house was overcrowded, it was hot and tempers were short. On that day I remember the last thing I was prepared to do was deal with the very adult emotions that I was being forced to deal with.

Overhearing my own mother talk about me like I was some dog in the street was the last straw that day. Everything came crashing down on me like a ton of bricks. I remember walking into the room where she was and saying "don't worry mother, you'll never have to worry about me again." I then proceeded to go into the bathroom and take so many pills that they began to come out of my nose, and then I collapsed.

To my young mind I would've rather been dead than face the reality of my life.

The incidence of people dying each year because of a drug overdose has climbed steadily. The Center for Disease Control reports that drug overdose deaths have increased 102 percent between the years of 1999 to 2010. Approximately 40 percent of those come as a result of illicit drug use. In the black community that number is even higher, but accurate figures aren't yet available.

But God had a different plan for me.

My suicide attempt was not successful. After being rushed to the hospital they revived me, gave me medicine and nursed me back to health. I don't remember how long I was there but I do remember that everyone there was so nice to me, even my parents. It was strange, but a welcome relief from my home life.

You would think that this would've been a wake-up call to not only me but to my entire family. Here I was, a young, single mother under the age of 16 who had just tried to take her own life. Was it a cry for help? Absolutely.
Did anyone listen?
No, including me.

This is where my life jumped from the frying pan and into the fire.

CHAPTER 10

HOT PANTS

And the God of all grace, who called you to his eternal glory in Christ, after you have suffered a little while, will himself restore you and make you strong, firm and steadfast. To him be the power for ever and ever. Amen.
1 Peter 5:10

When I was 15 years old I was the victim of a violent gang rape. For years I blocked it out of my memory. Not until recently have I begun to remember small details.

I was in the car with a bunch of men. I don't remember why, but there I was in an extremely vulnerable situation. All of a sudden everything went terribly wrong. The next thing I remember was seeing a car drive away from my limp body that lay atop a dusty mound in the empty Nevada desert. I'm sure they thought I was dead because they didn't drive off in a hurry.

You don't ever believe that something really bad can happen to you until it's too late. You hear stories all the time on the news about bad things happening to other people but never imagine that you could be that victim.

On that day I was the victim. After I got myself together (as good as I could) I somehow summoned enough strength in my legs to get up and walk. I don't know for how long I stumbled through the dark, lonely desert but eventually I saw the lights from a single house sitting in the distance. I was still very scared and in a lot of pain, but something inside told me that if I could make it to that house that I would be alright.

When I got to the door of the house I furiously knocked on the door hoping someone was there. A man opened the door and saw me. My heart began to race because of what had just happened. Would he too take advantage of me? At this point I didn't even care. It didn't matter what happened to me. Inside there were other men. I didn't know what to do. I was too weak to run. I was at their mercy.

But these men were different. They immediately helped me. Once he saw that I was in distress he and the other men took me in, helped clean me up, gave me water and then drove me back to my house. They didn't leave me until they saw I was in the house with my people.

I never saw those men again, but on that terrible night they saved my life.

I know it doesn't seem like it, but to my very young mind at the time there was one area of my life that I excelled in, and that area was men. They liked me and I liked them. They were easy, and predictable. I knew just what to do when I wanted them around (likewise I knew how to make them leave me alone.) I was never at a loss for their attention and there were plenty of them to choose from.

At the age of 16 most young girls are thinking about going to the prom or getting their first job or graduating from high school. That wasn't the case with me.

By the time I was 16 I already had two children. In my mind I was grown, so I figured that it was time to calm down enough to start thinking about getting married. There was already a guy who had already figured out that I was supposed to be his wife, and he was willing to wait. He was good to me and my children, and yes, I loved him. It made sense at that point in my life to go ahead and become his wife.

I know what you're thinking. Why would I want to be married when the only example of marriage that I had was so dysfunctional and destructive. The answer is not easy, nor does it make a lot of sense. As a young girl it was always in my mind that the natural state of a married couple was happiness. When an adult said "I'm married", I always thought they had access to a secret world where, in spite of their hardships, everybody was still more or less happy. Why else would they stay together? I wanted to be a member of that world so badly that by the age of 16 I had convinced myself that I was ready.

My future husband-to-be was 10 years older than me. I can only imagine that he saw a young, inexperienced and somewhat gullible younger woman who he could easily control. Because of my age I had to get my parent's approval and permission, which they gave me. With that out the way there was nothing to stop us. I was ready and so was he. Most importantly we wanted to do what we believed to be the right thing.

When we finally got married I was so excited. The thought of actually being someone's wife felt right to me. It felt natural. I was happy and content. Finally I had what I wanted.

Soon after, like so many women, I figured that the best way to show my love to my new husband was to have his child. It didn't take long. Soon we welcomed a little girl into the world, and now our family of 5 was complete and everything was good.

Sadly that's not how things worked out.

Shortly after we married and I was pregnant my husband started verbally abusing me. With ten years between us I'm sure that he grew impatient with me not doing everything he wanted me to do. We would get into these big arguments over a lot of different things, some big, some small.

Looking back the stress of being newly married with two kids and one on the way and not having a lot of money probably took its toll. Being that I came from an extremely dysfunctional background I didn't know how to be a mother and a wife. (I really didn't have any business being married in the first place.) Plus I had been abused while I lived at home, being powerless to do anything about it. There was no way that I was going to take that kind of abuse from a man who called himself my husband.

All of that, combined with the fact that I was still very young, became too much for the both of us. After I had our little girl the abuse became physical and before I knew it I had duplicated my parent's relationship.

I wasn't happy, nor was he. Our marriage had become more like a prison and, at once, I regretted ever doing it in the first place. I had grown to a point where I didn't even like him, let alone love him.

Again, he was 10 years older than me. I fully expected him to pack up and leave. He didn't have to stay. I wouldn't have even been mad if I had come home one day and all his stuff was gone. But that never happened. He never left. He stayed and said he wanted to work things out.

The funny thing was while he didn't want to leave me it didn't make me not want to leave him, which is exactly what I did after the abuse became so bad at home. I had grown tired of the endless cycle of physical and emotional violence that I was willing to do anything to separate myself from him. I wanted to protect my three young children, and I also wanted to have some of my own piece of mind.

So, guess what I did?

I left Las Vegas and moved to Cincinnati, Ohio. Yup, the kids and I packed up and moved to the rugged mid-west. With my marriage in trouble I felt like I didn't have anything worth staying for in Las Vegas. I had stopped attending school as now I had three kids and a husband to take care of. School was the last thing on my mind (this is another example of a bad decision that I don't blame anyone else but myself for).

You might be scratching your head and asking "out of all the places in the country you could've moved, what made you pick Cincinnati?" It would be nice to say that I went because of a job or because of family. After all,

Cincinnati was so different than the hot desert outpost of Las Vegas.

But those weren't the only reasons that I left Las Vegas with my three young children.

The main reason that I left was because I was chasing after another man. You see, while my marriage was becoming more unbearable by the day I met another man who I began to share a lot of my emotions with.

Like anything, it all began very innocently. I enjoyed all the attention he was giving to me. He would tell me things I wanted to hear, things that a woman would respond to. I started feeling like maybe we had something more than just talking to one another. I felt like he really wanted me to be with him. I definitely wanted to be with somebody who wanted me.

A lot of women in desperate situations do this, thinking that their answer is in the warm, protective arms of another man who says they love her and her children. It always winds up being completely different once she settles in and the day to day very unromantic reality sets in, at least to the man.

The bible says that the lord protects fools and babies. He had his hands full with me and I wasn't a baby.

Eventually after about 6 months I realized that I had made a terrible mistake. I missed my family back in Las Vegas and Cincinnati, Ohio was far too cold for a desert girl like me. All of these things combined let me know that whatever it was that I was searching for wasn't there.

I had to get back Vegas as quickly as possible.

When I pulled back into my home city and showed up on my husband's doorstep, much to my surprise he wasn't exactly excited to see me. With three children in tow I swallowed my pride and asked him to take me back, which he did.

Even though we were back together things between us didn't get any better. I was too self-absorbed in my own mess to get it.

I remember one day we wound up getting into a big fight about something. I don't even remember what it was now, but we were arguing and it got physical. He called me outside to continue fighting. In the midst of our physical battle I began to feel physically threatened and did the unthinkable: I pulled out a gun and shot him, twice.

By the grace of God he didn't die. On the other hand I got arrested and put into protective custody away from his family. My mother had to come and take custody of my children. I was only 17 years old, and with my birthday only a few days away, I wound up spending my 18th birthday in juvenile hall.

Over those 4 days locked-up, away from my family, I realized that something had to change. I couldn't continue to go down this path. The problem was I hadn't been equipped with the knowledge of how to take the steps necessary to turn my life around. Again, during this time I wasn't leading a godly life and had no one to turn to.

Still, God had his hand of protection on me. I believe very strongly that He guided the bullets away from any of my husband's vital organs. I could've killed him, but at that time I was wild and out of control.

After I got out and got my kids back I still had to deal with the legal residue that my actions caused. There was still a restraining order against me that kept me from being around him or his family. It wasn't until we were in court that I saw him again for the first time.

When he saw me for the first time since the incident had occurred he was still very angry. He walked up to me and slapped me in the face so hard that my nose began to bleed. My attorney rushed me to the bathroom to clean me up. When the judge entered the courtroom the bailiff, who had seen the entire thing unfold, told him what happened to me. The judge dismissed the case.

Again, God's hand of protection was on me, in spite of my own stupidity.

(Healing comes from a position of truth. That being said, due to the mature graphic nature of this chapter please read with care. It is my desire that someone is helped by something that is spoken. We need to break down the strongholds that keep us in bondage by being honest about demonic forces in our lives.)

CHAPTER 11

A Cry from the Heart

"Then they cried to the Lord in their trouble, and he saved them from their distress. He sent out his word and healed them; he rescued them from the grave."
Psalm 107:19-20

A Cry from the Heart

In the movie *The Passion of the Christ*, there is a scene where Jesus is flogged by the Roman guards. It is a heart-wrenching scene because of the extreme graphic nature in which it was filmed.

In this scene Jesus had been apprehended by the Pharisees and turned over to the Roman prelate, or governor, Pontius Pilate. At this point the Pharisees wanted Jesus to die because, they claimed, he was arousing Israel against Rome. The Pharisees pleaded with Pontius Pilate to crucify him, but Pilate refused and instead ordered Jesus to be whipped, or flogged, 40 times.

To the modern day reader of this ancient text we understand that flogging must have been a pretty severe punishment. The Romans were a very well organized people and surely they designed punishments that would deter people from breaking their laws. After all who

A Cry from the Heart

would want to be whipped 40 times in the public square? It sounds painful indeed, but definitely something that our 21st century minds could fathom as being survivable.

Enter Mel Gibson and his penchant for being a director who appreciates hyper-realism. Everyone who has seen this movie learned that the Roman soldiers who whipped Jesus tied jagged sea shells and shards of metal into their whips. Everyone who has seen this movie saw how they tested the effectiveness of their whips by striking a wooden table and watching the pieces of sea shells and metal bits stick into the wood. Everyone who has seen the movie watched the Roman guards tie Jesus to the whipping post and everyone who has seen the movie watched the first strike of the whip on Jesus's back violently rip flesh and muscle from his back.

But as crude and vicious of an attack as this was, the fact remained that he was ordered to receive 40 lashes. After what seemed like an eternity of unfathomable agony and pain they stopped beating him, only to turn him over and whip the front of his body while his hands were tied above his head. Thankfully the director didn't show the flesh being torn from his torso and face. It would've been too much.

What I'm about to tell you is like when they turned Jesus over and whipped the front of him.

I come from a family with a lot of siblings. Often times, as we got older we would get together and reminisce about when we were younger. I, being the eldest sister, had witnessed all of their births and thus had more history that I could share with them all. The problem was that I often didn't remember a lot of the same events that they remembered.

"Don't you remember when so and so came over to visit us," they'd say.

"No, I don't remember that at all."

Puzzled, they'd reply, "how come you don't remember it when you were right there with us?"

At first I would start to get upset with them, which wasn't hard for me, because I thought they were making it up. All of these so-called events that I was witness to but somehow didn't remember now that I was older must've never happened. I had always prided myself on the ability I had to recall things from when I was a young age. But now, according to them, I was missing out on an entire swath of time that they all remembered quite vividly.

What could this be and why?

I was starting to become concerned because the more they seemed to bring up the less I was able to remember.

"Don't you remember when so and so would come by and stay with us for a while?"

"No."

"What? He would come by and play with us and bring us stuff."

"I don't remember," I'd say.

"What? He really liked you. He was always asking for you when he came around," they'd say.

I didn't remember anyone from my childhood except my mother. I remember how much I wanted her to love me and show me that she cared. I remember always tip-toeing around the house so that I wouldn't make her mad. I remember always wondering what it would feel like to hear her say "I love you."

It was then that I began to pray to the Lord and ask Him to help me remember certain events of my childhood. I was starting to become concerned that something was really wrong with me. I didn't want to believe that I was beginning to lose my mind.

The fact that my siblings could remember more about my childhood than I could persisted for some time, and it really began to bother me. It bothered me to the point of it always being an earnest prayer request.

Eventually God's answer made it to me, just like it did to Daniel when he prayed about the king's vision and didn't receive an immediate response. In the book of Daniel chapter 10 it explains how Daniel had to wait 21 days for the angel Gabriel to get a message to him. I can't remember how long I had to wait, but it was longer than 21 days. I never doubted that God would answer my prayers, but I knew that it would happen in His own time. He knew what was on my heart and how badly I wanted to remember parts of my childhood that I had obviously forgotten about. Maybe there were some good memories after all.

Unfortunately, it was quite the contrary. By this time I was older and God knew that I was able to process the reality of my past I began to remember events, and they were terrible.

At the age of 5 years old I had been a victim of sexual molestation by a close male family member.

At first the memories were slow to materialize. I remembered being at a bar with a man. His face was never fully revealed to me in my memory. As I concentrated on the memory of the bar and the man, God began to reveal more and more of what had actually occurred on that very sad day.

Selective memory is a coping mechanism by which the victim, in this case me, is best able to deal with a traumatic situation. It is a form of amnesia and addresses two areas of memory that everyone has: passive versus active memory. Passive memory is an action where you don't really know if your memory was engaged when you were doing it, like laying your keys down while concentrating on something else. Active memory means that your memory was fully engaged when you were doing something, like handling a skillet with hot oil in it.

When you don't want to remember something, usually something traumatic, selective memory is where that information goes. It is tucked deep behind the vault of your active memory. Often times it is through selective memory that demons can form their most lethal and long lasting strongholds.

When I was 5 years old this very close male family member took me to a bar and sat me atop where the drinks were served. I didn't know what was going on. I thought he wanted to show me off. I was so proud of the outfit I was wearing. It made me feel pretty, and special. But that's not what he had on his mind. His evil obsession had finally reached its boiling point and he could no longer control himself. He took me home, away from anyone else's eyes who might tell, and proceeded to put his hand down my panties and fondled me. He didn't penetrate me, but I do remember his big, rough fingers feeling around my private parts. Instinctually, even as a child, I pushed his hand away and he stopped.

Even then I knew it was wrong for me to be in a place where there were only grown-ups. There were no other children around anywhere. It was dark and for a child it was very scary being in a bar where people were all watching.

And just like that, he stole my innocence and in the process, unbeknownst to me, opened up a window that overtook the both of us.

In the book of Ephesians the apostle Paul states "for our struggle is not against flesh and blood, but against the rulers, against the authorities, against the powers of this dark world and against the spiritual forces of evil in the heavenly realms."

If you're not convinced of that and would rather take a more scientific approach to understanding pathology, there is a scientific term called reactive psychosis. This mental disorder is triggered by a recognizably traumatic life event, in my case rape and relationships. In other words a person is more than likely to have a negative reaction when faced with the same type of events that caused the psychosis in the first place.

Being fondled at such a young age completely throws a young woman's life spiraling out of control. It is not uncommon for many victims of this form of abuse to have a hard time expressing intimacy, both physical and or emotional. Thoughts of suicide start to arise because of the damage to your own self-worth. It begins a vicious cycle of destruction.

When abusers commit these lewd acts on children what it does is open a spiritual door where evil can come in and wreak havoc on the life of the participant. The confusion that follows isn't always related to the type of activity that invited the evil in the first place. Once evil has a place at the table of your soul it can, and does, start to make itself at home in other areas of your life too.

Rape is one of the most violently offensive forms of evil that exists. It is not just a physical act. It is the spiritual, physical and mental violation of one person by another person. When there's a child involved the stakes are even higher because now you've tarnished a future of someone else in a matter of seconds.

Nationally 1 in 6 boys will be sexually assaulted before the age of 18 while 1 in 4 girls will be. Most of the time the perpetrator is a close family member or friend. Usually the victimizer has some form of power over their victim.

I don't really remember any of the emotions I had regarding that event. I was so very young, plus I pushed it so far out of my mind that the only thing I remembered was fuzzy at best. But I do know that it happened.

I'd like to say that it only happened once, but sadly it occurred several other times that I can finally remember.

One time my parents were having one of their drinking parties at our house. I could tell everyone was starting to get a little tipsy because the music and the laughter were starting to get louder. I remember seeing my mother smiling, having a good time with some of her friends. It wasn't often that I saw her smile, but on this occasion I did. Even though she did everything she could do to push me away from her, I still experienced the youthful joy of seeing momma happy.

We only had one bathroom in our small apartment, and I had to go really bad. When it was empty I walked over to the door and shut it behind me before anyone got there. Our bathroom wasn't too big. There wasn't much room to move around in, and me being so little it still seemed crowded. We had a bathtub, the one we used to wash sheets in, a sink that both of my parents used and a toilet. There was a shower curtain hanging around the bathtub.

As I prepared to use the bathroom, all of a sudden the door swung open and he walked in. My stomach tightened in a knot as I instinctively reached down to pull up my panties. He moved closer to me as I backed away, not knowing what he was trying to do. I was going to start yelling but again, I didn't want to get in trouble for being loud and ruining

A Cry from the Heart

my parent's party. My mother wouldn't have wasted the opportunity to blame me for messing up her party with my screams.

So I remained silent as he inched his large, hulking body towards mine. I tried to get a view of the bathroom door to see if I could escape. Again, he was a large man and blocked my way. I couldn't even see the door.

By now he was standing over me, and I was very nervous. "What did he want" I wondered. I hadn't completely pushed out of my memory what he had done to me a few years earlier. But we had seen each other since then at family events and he didn't act like that anymore. He didn't even pay much attention to me anymore. So when I had seen him show up to my parent's party tonight I didn't think twice about turning my back on him.

And that was my first mistake. The old saying that a leopard never changes his spots is true. Looking back on it I guess he just waited until the right circumstances presented themselves again. He had probably been looking at me the entire evening waiting for the right moment to pounce like the predator he was. When he saw me go to the bathroom he immediately went into action to execute his devilish plan.

Again it was the same thing. He put his hands down my panties and fondled me. I was in shock. I didn't know what to say because he was very close to my family and everyone loved him. He had always been nice to us as kids and, well, no one listened to me anyway so they wouldn't believe me if I did say anything. These are the words that ran through my mind while he was there with me in the bathroom. Eventually I pushed his hands away from me and he left, closing the door behind him. There I sat in the bathroom, alone. I couldn't believe what had just happened. I felt afraid and angry. "Why isn't anyone here to protect me? Where are all the adults? Why does he always do this to me? What am I doing to make him act this way?"

I was only 9 years old.

Parents, please watch your children. Never turn your back on them. The sexual predators are out there watching and waiting for the perfect opportunity to strike. Once they strike they leave a stain behind and a spiritual window opened. Being diligent about your children's well-being will spare them a lifetime of hurt and shame. Believe me, if someone had watched out for me there's no way that the same thing would've happened a third time.

At the age of 14 I already had my first child. My life was spiraling out of control. I was full of anger because of my home life. I didn't trust anyone because there were no adults in my immediate world who had ever helped or protected me from harm. In a word I was a hot mess.

By now my mother's resentment towards me had grown to a boiling point. Looking back on it I now understand why. I believe that she knew I was being molested. Again, she knew the guy. We all did. She saw the change in my behavior whenever he would come around. I never said anything, but a mother always knows when there's something wrong with their child, especially their little girl.

But when I was younger I never received any clue that she knew or that she cared. She never came to me in private and asked me if something was wrong. I would've told her. I would've told anyone who would've listened. The problem was that no one cared enough to ask, including her. So, I was truly alone.

Whenever this male family member would come over her demeanor would change for the worst. She became really belligerent with me and would go out of her way to say mean things to me. Strangely when this family member wasn't around she acted as if she was oblivious to my whereabouts or my well-being. I was treated with complete indifference.

This particular afternoon though my mother's anger towards me had hit an all-time high. I remember that she awoke me from my sleep. In actuality she was beating me awake with something in her hand. I don't know if it was a belt or something else, but she was completely out of control.

"I hate you! I can't stand you. Get out of my house, get out right now!"

"What did I do, what did I do," I yelled as I frantically scrambled to get away from her blows. Every other strike seemed to land and I was moving as fast as I could after having been violently awakened from sleeping. Sadly this wasn't the first time she had done this to me. I was used to this kind of abuse.

Her berating continued and it was so bad that I wound up feeling like committing suicide was my only option. I had already had a child and the reality of being a single young mother was too much to handle, coupled with the fact that home as more like a prison. So I went out to meet this woman who sold drugs and I bought some from her with the intention of coming back home and overdosing.

Wouldn't you know, I couldn't even get that part right. And while I didn't die I did give myself one of the most mind numbing highs that I had ever experienced. I could barely stand up straight. I walked into the next room where my mother was and she exploded on me with a rage I had never seen before. She started yelling and calling me names. It was awful.

A Cry from the Heart

I wound up leaving home that night just to get away from her. I had reached the point where I simply couldn't take it anymore.

But where was I to go? Here I was, 14 years old, high as a kite walking the streets of Las Vegas at night. Anything could've happened to me, but somehow I made my way to one of the other woman's places where I knew one of my close male relatives stayed sometimes. I knocked on the door and he was there and let me in. I'm sure I surprised him as I stood there asking him for a place to stay. He offered me the couch and then he disappeared to one of the back rooms.

I don't know how much time had passed but when I awoke he was on top of me. No longer was I some little girl wearing pigtails and dresses. Now I was a 14 year-old single mother who had been abused by several men in her life. I guess he figured I was a woman now and "just" fondling was no longer going to satisfy his appetite. In his own twisted mind he had been secretly grooming me for a time such as this. He fully penetrated me this time. And because of who he was I was frozen with fear and shame, just like I had been when I was a little baby girl. I was so high that I couldn't fight him off, but I do remember trying to reach up with my hands.

"Stop it. This is not right. We should not be doing this," I remember saying as he assaulted me. Those were the only words I had the courage to say. He didn't listen. The assault continued until he was done, and then he left as I just lay there alone with a mountains worth of shame. My shoulders were not strong enough to carry the load, even though, at the time, I thought I was tough enough to handle anything that came my way. It was my youthful folly, my attempt to act like it didn't matter.

But it did matter. I noticed that a slow and deliberate transformation was beginning to occur in my life. All of the rich colors in my life started to slowly morph into black and white shadows that hid themselves in the darkest and deepest chasms of my mind. Where there was once life there was now just varying shades of gray. I found solace in the grays because gray is in the middle, and in the middle it was safe.

It was then that I found my coping mechanism.
Forgetting.

The only way that I could continue to move forward was to forget about the entire trauma, especially the rape. It was too much of a burden to constantly relive, so I pretended like it never happened. Even though it's destruction was all encompassing in my life, as long as I didn't think about it I was okay.

As much as I didn't want to admit it, the anger that was blossoming inside of me was because I never honestly dealt with the shame and the guilt. I was ashamed of having been a victim of something so horrible and couldn't help but feel that if the adults of my life had been more diligent and taken their roles as protectors more seriously that none of this would've happened. A lot of my rage came from that fact alone. Why didn't they protect me?

Parents, please, protect your children. Let them know that you're there and that you have their backs. Guard their innocence. Do not expect them to process adult situations and adult emotions like an adult would. They're children. Allow them to enjoy their childhood. They'll be adults far longer than they'll be children. Don't rob them of that.

The other reason that I was so angry was because of my guilt. Deep in my mind, and because there were no adults there to tell me otherwise, I always felt like it was my fault. I felt that somehow I was to blame for what happened to me. Nothing could be further from the truth. It is NEVER a victim's fault that they were assaulted. No matter what people would like to say to the opposite, the victim is never the person who is at fault. They're the victim, plain and simple.

It took me years to understand this simple fact. It wasn't my fault. A woman is often hard pressed to acknowledge that something inherent in her femininity causes a man to act like that. Nothing could be further from the truth. Men who use that as an excuse are not men at all.

The time that I spent actively placing all of my hurts and sorrows in the secret hiding place of my mind could've been spent doing something much more productive, like learning how to make decisions that would help my life instead of destroying it further.

But God hadn't had the last word yet.

CHAPTER 12

EMPTIED TO BE USED FOR GOD'S GLORY

"For a brief moment I abandoned you, but with deep compassion I will bring you back. In a surge of anger I hid my face from you for a moment, but with everlasting kindness I will have compassion on you," says the Lord your Redeemer."
Isaiah 54:7-9

God's tests always accompany His promises. This is the part of the Christian life that, I believe, chases most people away.

The world would often have you believe that you have to be tough in order to be a part of it. You always hear terms like "dog eat dog" or "survival of the fittest" when the attributes of successful people are described. In the world of the streets the colder and more diabolical you were translated into more success. It was truly the code of the streets. In my own life if you stepped up to me talking crazy I was going to swing first and talk second. That was my mantra.

I was tough by the world's standards. I had earned my stripes and nobody messed with me. I knew the streets and the streets knew me.

I can now see God was smiling in amusement of my bravado. Here I was thinking

I was tough because I made sure that people respected me out of fear. When I turned my life over to the Lord I soon found out that I wasn't tough at all. In fact I found out that I was quite the opposite.

In Genesis when God was establishing a relationship with Abram (later to become Abraham) he told him to leave his father's household and to go out to a land that He would tell him to possess. When Abram left his father's house he didn't know where he was going. The city where he lived, Ur, was a large city. Abram had lived there his entire life, so it's what he knew. Most researchers agree that there were about 50,000 inhabitants there. This was no small outpost, and for Abram to up and leave and go into the great unknown was a big deal.

Likewise when I decided to leave behind the life that I knew, the only life that I had grown up with, it was scary. It took me awhile to grasp ahold of the idea that I was going to be relying on someone other than myself for total direction and comfort. Being vulnerable in my life was not a good place for me as I had been taken advantage of in the worst possible way on several occasions. Trusting in someone else did not come easy, especially because I had never seen it done in any of my immediate circles.

Going to church and dedicating my life to helping move the Lord's kingdom forward was not easy. At first I was truly a foreigner in a foreign land. I didn't know how to act "churchy", and by that I mean speaking in King James English and knowing what verses to recite. I was raw and vulnerable. But thankfully God's people took me under their wing and loved me in spite of myself.

My home life was much better. My grandson was the apple of my eye, my daughter had recovered and my marriage, even though it still had its occasional struggles, was still intact.

Emptied to be Used for God's Glory

My church family had taken me in, cleaned me up and helped me to become a woman of God. The family that I had always wanted was beginning to grow and prosper. At last, we were in a good place.

Abram was in a similar place in Genesis 15. God told him to not be afraid (which was the first time this command was mentioned in the bible). Why would Abram be afraid? By now Abram had a wife, he had land, he had wealth, and he had the favor of one of the local rulers. To the human mind and eye Abram had it going on. But still God told him to not be afraid because He, the Lord, was his shield, his very great reward. Since God lives outside of the time space continuum I believe that God knew what Abram didn't know, and that was the fact that Abram was about to go through a test. The bible clearly states that Abram wanted a son, an heir that would carry on his name and household. But God told him that his offspring would outnumber the stars in the sky.

So God then told Abram to "bring me a heifer, a goat and a ram, each three years old, along with a dove and a young pigeon." In the next verse it tells us that "Abram brought all of these to Him, cut them in two and arranged the halves opposite each other." During this time when people entered into covenants with one another they would cut animals in half and spread them apart leaving a row between the halves. The two parties entering the covenant together would pass down the aisle in between the two cut halves, thus solidifying the covenant between them.

In that culture a covenant was more binding than a contract. In today's society legally there is a distinction between a covenant and a contract. It's very simple; a contract spells out obligations and limitations. If either party doesn't live up to their obligations the contract is deemed to be null and void. A covenant is different, it's a vow. It says that no matter what

I'm still obligated to do everything that I said I would do.

God is not interested in entering into contracts with us; he's only interested in covenants. Why? Because you don't enter into a contract with someone you want to become intimate with. God longs for intimacy with us, and in order to do that he has to perform surgery on our hearts. Like any good surgeon, the first thing God has to do is make an incision so that He can get to the problem. Like the two halves of the slaughtered animals, He had to cut into Abram's heart to get into the part of his inner being where intimacy was.

Likewise, God had to cut into my heart so that he could be intimate with me. He wanted to go into that place of deep pain and hurt, insecurity, the need to be loved, the scars of victimization and abuse that I had suffered and hid behind drugs and men. He wanted to go into that dark, hollow place that I had buried behind the new mask of holiness that I was wearing. He wanted to get into my bad stuff.

And you know what? I thought I had spent years proving how tough I was to everyone around me. After I was through convincing them I started to convince myself of how tough I was. I had myself convinced too. I knew there was no one as tough on the inside as me. At least that was until God showed me that I was a big chicken. While I did know that I needed His help, I wasn't too sure if I was willing to be that transparent and that….naked. But, just like Abram whom God entered into a covenant with while he was asleep, God had also entered into a covenant with me when I first called His name.

There were some things that I hid from all of my new found church family that I was ashamed of. They were ugly things. True, my grandson had been a huge blessing to me. It was his birth that drove me to the Lord in the first place. Still, worshipping God is not safe if you're not willing to give something up as a sacrifice. Worship always has a cost.

One of the biggest things that I used to be ashamed of was my drug use. I had repented of it when I gave my life to the Lord after my grandson was born. I knew that I couldn't be any type of role model to him or to anyone else if this habit continued to plague me. And while I would never admit to being an addict, as I had always equated addicts with not being able to control their obsessions, my use, prior to repenting, was more than just recreational. It had become part of my life.

It had become an idol.

Still, after I had accepted the Lord into my life my husband was still abusing crack cocaine. He knew of my new life in Christ but that didn't stop him from wanting me to continue using it with him. I told him no, that I was freed from my past addictions, and that I wouldn't be using it anymore. He persisted, and I continued to say no.

Just like the story in Genesis about Abram preparing the sacrifice to the Lord, birds of prey tried swooping down to take the animal halves that he had prepared as a direct result of the Lord's instructions. Abram had to fight off those birds because the sacrifice did not belong to them. Likewise I had to fight off the constant pleading of my husband to take drugs with him. The sacrifice I was making wasn't for him anyway. It was for the Lord, my grandson, my daughter, and our family. Like Abram I wanted to insure that my sacrifice was not tampered with.

I'd like to say that, like Abram, I was successful in warding off the vultures that were coming to take God's sacrificial offering away. In Chapter 15, verse 11 it clearly states that Abram was successful.

I wasn't.

Five months had passed since I had taken any drugs. One evening my husband came home and was, like always, about to smoke the crack cocaine in our rear bedroom. I was in the front of our house because I knew what he was doing and didn't want to have any part of it. This evening I felt exceptionally vulnerable for some reason, like I was going to go and join him. Eventually I gave into my feelings and went in the back room and we wound up smoking together, 10 rocks of crack cocaine.

Immediately the Holy Spirit convicted me of my wrongdoing and I felt horrible. I repented to God and promised to never do it again. I know God heard me because the Word of God says that he is just to forgive us of our sins if we repent. I had rebelled against the one who had saved me from certain death, just like the children of Israel did. I was no better than they were.

The next day my pastor's mother called me and said "God said to say he knows what you did last night and don't do it anymore."

The only possible way my pastor's mom knew what I had done the night before was that the Holy Spirit had revealed it to her. My husband never talked to any of my church family and I hadn't told anyone. We smoked the drugs in the privacy of our own home. No one saw anything. I was extra convicted of my actions because now I couldn't even hide from God the very thing that I was going to be hiding from people. Surely he wanted my heart, the part that I hid from everyone else. He wanted to break me in that place that made me want to find solace in drugs in the first place. He said, "I am your solace. I am your peace. Invite me in and I will make your life new."

So you know what I did? I eventually got caught up in the same snare again, smoking crack with my husband. Part of the reason I did it was because I knew, deep down within, that if I didn't share in this activity with him that he wouldn't love me anymore. I felt like leaving that life, while it would've been the best thing for me to do, would've alienated me from the love I had grown accustomed to receiving from him.

God was showing me that He didn't want just a piece of me, He wanted all of me, everything that I was hiding from everyone else He saw and He wanted.

Still, I rebelled. I was going through the motions at church. I was still ushering. I never stopped believing that God was a healer, but this layer of emotional and spiritual intimacy that God was requiring of me I wasn't yet ready for. I wanted God but then I didn't want Him all in my "business." Little did I know at the time that the intimacy He wanted from me was more fulfilling than the intimacy I sought from any other man, including my husband.

There were two other times that I used drugs with my husband, and each time the Holy Spirit convicted my heart that what I was doing was hurtful to God. Both times my pastor's mother called me and delivered the same message to me. I didn't listen. I was hard-headed and afraid.

After the second time of using crack my husband and I got into a fierce argument and, once again, the same pattern of abuse that I had experienced as a child returned on me as he began to physically assault me. I fought back as hard as I could, mostly to protect myself, but he definitely had the upper hand.

As fate would have it my son came by the house and saw that he had beat me up pretty badly. He went to my husband and said "did you do this to my mama?" and then he proceeded to beat my husband until they had both run out into the street. My son was beating him so badly that a crowd of people had to pull him off my husband and call the ambulance. When they arrived they called another ambulance to take both him and me to the hospital. That's how badly he beat me and my son had beaten him. We spent the night in the same hospital but in different rooms.

As I lay there in the bed I replayed the warning of my pastor's mother over and over inside my head. I knew that I had done wrong in the sight of the Lord. I felt just like the children of Israel being punished with 400 years of captivity in Egypt. My injuries were my immediate consequence to the rabid disobedience I had shown to God's instructions. It was then that I realized that God loved me more than my addiction. I learned that His covenant with me didn't depend on me holding up my end, that He loved me in spite of me.

It was then that I knew God had a bigger purpose for me than hiding the fact that I was still using drugs. Right there, in that hospital

Emptied to be Used for God's Glory

room, I fully surrendered to Him that part of me that I was hiding in shame. He came in a filled the void in my heart that wanted the drugs in the first place. I never had a desire for them after that.

In fact, the Lord made it very plain for me that my ministry would begin immediately after I got out of the hospital. He told me that I would be a minister of the gospel after I was released. This was a long way away from the life that I had been seemingly programmed for. This was a culmination of all of my prayers, that God would use me to help people. I was so excited and couldn't wait to get started.

As far as my relationship with my husband went, after we were both released from the hospital things were never quite the same. All of the changes that had been going on in my life were too much for him to handle. I never forced my new lifestyle on him and he never expressed any interest in joining me in my new walk.

My intuition had been telling me for some time that he had been seeing another woman. Had I not been anchored in my faith by now this fact would've driven me back into some self-destructive habits. It pained me to see that what we had together was falling apart before our eyes. It didn't feel good on the day he left me for good to go and be in her arms. It was a very sad time in my life.

Thank God I had my new church family to help me to stay strong. They provided a much needed spiritual and emotional support network as I once again navigated the waters of being single again. Of course I felt all of the emotions associated with being left for another woman. I don't want you to think that I didn't experience all of the pain and bitterness that comes from rejection that any woman would feel. It took a lot of prayer to get me through that very difficult time.

The major difference this time was that now I had a grandchild who I loved and adored. I had a daughter who desperately needed my attention and a son who was showing signs of drifting into a life of crime. My hands were full at home and now I was going to have to do it without the support of a husband.

Throughout this entire ordeal I walked away knowing that God loved me and that He wanted to have an intimate relationship with me. He wanted to provide for me unlike any man or anything had provided for me in my entire life. Overcoming my addictions and some of my fears had been as simple as fully surrendering to Him. Once I got ME out of the way things became a lot easier. I started to grow in grace and God began to use me in ways that I would've never imagined. My life took on a whole new meaning as my zeal for Him grew.

Revelation 3:19 says "those whom I love I rebuke and discipline. So be earnest and repent." The Greek word used for discipline is paideuo, which means to train. The word also means "to chasten by the affliction of evils and calamities."

Like I said earlier I knew that God loved me. He sought an intimate relationship with me unlike any other before. I didn't understand it at the time but each calamity that befell me during my earlier life had ultimately moved me closer to Him. I was now in a place where I was able to better accept His desire to be first in my life, to be the one I turned to with all of my needs.

Still, I wasn't prepared for where he was going to take me next. Little did I know He was preparing me all along.

CHAPTER 13

I Changed Dance Partners

> *"Behold, I am making all things new."*
> ***Revelation 21:5***

There was little about my life now that resembled the past. God had transformed me in a way that it was only possible for Him to do. Had I been left to my own vices I would've surely killed myself by now, or somebody else.

My daughter was growing into her role as a young mother now that she had a child of her own. I was very deliberate in making sure that I could be there to support her as she was making this life-changing transition. Fortunately my job allowed me the time I wanted to be able to spend with her.

Throughout this time in her life I wanted to give her a level of emotional, psychological and spiritual support that I never received at her age. It was a very exciting time for the both of us as so many of the types of issues that a mother and daughter should share with one another were foreign to me. I am glad that God blessed me with a heart that was eager to understand everything she needed. Together we learned from one another, and it was wonderful. I was so proud of the young woman, and mother, she was growing up to be.

During those days my son was beginning to struggle with the reality that society didn't see him as a boy anymore, but rather a young black man. As much as I'd like to say that I understood what he was going through, I didn't. During some of his most formative years when a positive male role model would've done him a world of good I was too busy chasing after the wrong men for the wrong reasons. I was young and foolish and my decisions, I believe, forced him to grow up much sooner than he should've.

From a young age he had to secure his own emotional security from role models outside of our home. There were no men, good men around to steer and guide him on a path that wasn't destructive. But because they provided him with an emotional rescue that I, a young mother who didn't know a good man when she saw him, wasn't able to provide to him. Looking back on it, in a lot of ways, he was just like me when I was younger. We both gravitated towards the voices that paid us the most attention.

Trying to fight the streets, especially after they had established a stronghold in someone, is a very difficult thing to do. Having a child slowed me down, as it did my daughter. He was a young man and didn't have to worry about the concrete reality of having a child at a young age. Fortunately he hadn't, to the best of my knowledge, had any children by now. His vice was the streets and drugs, namely selling them. The prospect of fast cash was indeed very enticing, especially to a young man who sees all of his peers profiting from the same thing.

I spent many nights praying to God, asking him to protect my boy as he was daily bombarded with this dangerous reality.

Sometimes I lamented about my son's situation and would stress out over it. As a parent you always wish that you could do more to help your children. And while we had a good relationship, it was nowhere near as close to what my daughter and I had. Maybe it was because I could relate to her better as a woman. Maybe it was because of the fractured relationship I had with my parents and how that affected how I related with others, even my own children. After leaving home we never really reconciled. They were very loving towards their grandchildren, but when it came down to me nothing had really changed.

We were still estranged. At that time I had no feelings about it either way.

Many of the scars that I had endured as a result of my past life, both emotional and psychological, were beginning to heal. When I looked into the mirror at myself, the scared, lonely and emotionally fractured little girl I had been was becoming a thing further and further in the past. So many of the painful things I had experienced didn't haunt me anymore. I no longer defined myself by my past, but rather I looked towards the future as my most promising, and prominent, trait.

As I settled into my new life even my daily routine changed. I was now completely involved in nearly every aspect of my church. Where I had, at once, began as an usher, as a result of my faithfulness to God's word my pastor saw fit to slowly entrust me with more of the daily responsibilities of the church. I soon received a key to the church and was overseeing others. People could see that my zeal for the things of God was real and not an act. I enjoyed serving Him in all that I did. People on my job, people who I had been living that life with, my friends and family all recognized that the old me was quickly becoming a thing of the past.

It was all about the new me!

On one particular occasion my pastor asked me to travel to San Bernardino, California to accompany him and his wife as they preached at a church that invited him to speak.

The City of San Bernardino is located about an hour and a half east of Los Angeles and about a 3.5 hour drive from Vegas. I was glad to have impressed my pastor with my faithfulness at church and gladly obliged. Travelling with me I brought my new husband, my daughters and my young grandson. We made it into a little mini-trip to support him.

The church service we attended was great. My pastor was very well received by the people who attended. Afterwards we went to eat at a nice restaurant and then loaded up in our cars and began our trip back home.

I was very glad to have my family attend with me. Them seeing me operate within the church was very rewarding to me. Yes, while I spent many hours performing multiple duties at the church it was all for the sake of moving Gods kingdom forward. While I was still living in the world I had lived very hard. I wanted to live equally as committed in my new walk. Traveling to San Bernardino, therefore, became as much a part of mission work as it was having the privilege of serving my pastor.

The 15 freeway is the main artery that connects Southern California and Nevada. It starts in San Diego and ends at the Canadian border, just outside of Sweetgrass, Montana. I had traveled this route many times as both a child and an adult. When you travel it as much as I had there are certain physical landmarks that you create to let you know how close you are to home. Over my many trips I had inadvertently done the same thing. I knew that once we hit Baker, CA we had about another 1.5 hours to go.

Not much exists along that route once you get outside of Barstow, CA. It's pretty much all desert with an occasional rolling hill or rugged pass. Prior to it being paved and turned into an interstate, Native Americans had used what we now call the 15 freeway for trade and travel.

Not soon after driving through the city of Barstow, CA the 15 turns into a two lane highway in both the northern and southern direction. Separating these two is a large sandy median.

This would become very important.

Somewhere outside the city of Barstow, as my husband at the time is driving along our tire blows out and our car begins to go out of control. Immediately I started to pray, hoping that God wouldn't let him hit the brakes and the soft median would eventually stop us. Suddenly our car began to tumble and flip end over end until it stopped.

The next thing I remembered was awakening in a hospital bed. The doctors told me that when the car was flipping I hit my head on the windshield and somehow my hair got caught and subsequently pulled my scalp from my head. After being thrown from the car, they tell me, my left leg was broken in three places, my back was broken in four places, my nose was broken and the left side of my face was crushed to the point of them wanting to remove my left eye.

When I finally had the chance to speak with my pastor he told me that he and his wife had seen the entire accident as it was happening, and it was bad. He told me that at the crash site I was telling my husband to get off me.

Immediately my concern was with my grandson and daughters. Since I had been awake no one had spoken about them.

"How's Trivion (my grandson)," I asked. "How're my girls?"

There was silence in the room.
"They're fine," my pastor said.
"How's Trivion," I said. I was still groggy from all of the medication I was on, but I was beginning to become anxious. I wanted to know how my baby, my gift from God was doing.

My pastor hesitated, and I could tell from the look in his eyes that it wasn't going to be good news. Still, I needed to hear it.

"When the ambulance got there, they had to take Trivion from his mother's arms. They instinctively locked around his body. She wouldn't release him to the paramedics. She was in shock."

Still, I needed to hear it. My heart was beginning to sink in my chest as I was becoming more and more unsettled.

I Changed Dance Partners

Trivion died. He didn't make it.

Later I found out that my pastor had chosen not to come and see me because he knew that I would ask him about Trivion. As I had laid in the bed, under heavy medical sedation, I had been praying and the Lord told me to call him and let him know that God had already revealed to me, in my spirit, that my grandson was no longer with us. I refused God's command because I was so angry that here, after all that I had done for Him, He would take my grandson from me. I didn't want to talk to anyone.

In the natural I had actually misplaced my pastor's phone number, so I used that as an excuse as to why I had chosen to be disobedient to God's voice. It was then that He reminded me of my pastor's phone number, and eventually I broke down and called him.

"Hello," I said. At first he didn't recognize my voice. I was still on so much medication and my face was still very swollen. It was difficult to talk.

Eventually he realized it was me, and then there was nothing but silence on the other end.

"Where is Trivion," I asked him.

There was a long pause, a sigh, and then he spoke these words that I will never forget.

"What did God tell you?"

I said, "he is dead."

Just hearing the words come out of my own mouth was more than I could handle. I experienced an anguish and a deep despair that I had no words for. I couldn't be there to comfort my daughter. I would never be able to hold my grandbaby again. I didn't protect them at their most vulnerable time.

I couldn't handle it.

My heart sank and life didn't mean as much to me anymore. At that point I didn't care if I lived or if I died. My grandson was gone and it was all my fault. If I hadn't brought them along on the trip with me this wouldn't have happened. Why would God allow something like this to happen? Why would he take away the very thing that caused me to seek him in the first place?

In my spirit I became very angry with God for doing such a thing. I had been faithful in my walk, I had done the best I could and now He took away the most innocent, untainted and perfect object of my affection away from me. How could he be so cruel?

I was in the hospital from June 9th to July 4th. As my body began to heal I had a vision of my grandson in a little casket. He looked like an angel. I wanted to be there with him so bad, but the spirit of the Lord told me in that dream that I would not be attending his funeral. The next day, after the funeral, my daughter brought me a picture of him in his casket and it was the exact vision that God had shown me.

Eventually, and with much prayer, my body healed back to normal. My pastor's mother came and prayed for me and said God was going to heal me. My sister came and prayed for my back every day. In the end I didn't have to lose my left eye after all, and the doctors were used mightily of the Lord in repairing my broken leg, back and fractured skull.

During that same time God mended my broken heart. While I'll never understand why He allowed such a tragedy to occur I can now better understand how life can never be taken for granted. When people would come to see me as I was healing God was faithful to me and always gave me a word of encouragement for them. So many people were blessed and came to the Lord as a result of that tragedy. This led me to the conclusion that no matter how bad you might think that things are, the sweet gift of life is to be cherished and guarded for all that it is. Nothing even remotely compares to it.

After leaving the hospital The Lord allowed me to begin a series of transformative conversations with my parents. Our relationship is much stronger now and I've been able to tell them with all sincerity, that I love them and don't hold any grudges against them. Daily I am still being blessed in this area as God continues to heal me of so much pain and hurt that they caused me as a child. But God is bigger than any problem that I have. He is stronger than any stronghold that tries to take claim on me, and He is patient enough to love me in spite of my transgressions.

Through it all God has shown me that His love for me is real and that every good and perfect thing truly does come from above. While it hasn't been easy, mostly as a result of my own stubbornness, God has loved and kept me close to Him so that He can be glorified through my own weaknesses, pain and sorrow.

CHAPTER 14

THE GREAT RECOVERY

"I will repay you for the years the locusts have eaten, the great locust and the young locust, the other locusts and the locust swarm, my great army that I sent among you. You will have plenty to eat, until you are full, and you will praise the name of the Lord your God, who has worked wonders for you; never again will my people be shamed."

Joel 2: 25-26

The Great Recovery

The God of my creation never intended for me to be devoured by the field that he placed me in. And even though my life seemed to be one tragic event after another I am reminded of the purpose of the lowly caterpillar. Its job is to devour everything in its path. It needs every leaf, every vegetable, every fruit, every rose petal, every root, every insect it can get ahold of in order to grow.

From my early family life, through adolescence and young adulthood to my later years it seemed that my life was devouring me instead of me devouring it. It seemed overwhelming and I had no idea of exactly how I would end up. Sometimes just making it through the day was the best that I could do.

But it was just food for my next stage.

It was very hard and at times, yes, I didn't know if I had what it took to make it. But just like the children of Israel during their desert experience God sent me bread in the form of people and places. My grandmothers were a huge help to me when I was a young child. They planted a seed deep inside of my young and impressionable heart. I didn't know it at the time but their prayers and acts of kindness helped create a standard in me that would sustain me through some very hard times.

But it was just nutrients for my next stage.

As my walk with the Lord started to mature my pastor and his wife became invaluable resources of strength, honor and dignity. I had never known those attributes growing up the way that I did. They will never know how much their presence in my life changed me for the better.

I know this may sound strange, but I thank God for allowing me to go through what I went through. Of course I didn't think about it then like I do now, but had God not allowed me to experience the things that I experienced I would've never been able to have the compassion for people that I have now, especially towards those that lived as I did. My heart literally bleeds for young unwed mothers who receive no support from their families. I know exactly how they feel and what they need. God has blessed me with a heart to listen and offer support, and for that I am truly thankful.

Now that I've grown in my spiritual walk and have met so many wonderful people, once they get to know a little more about what I've gone through (and believe me, there's a lot that I haven't talked about in this book) they all ask me the same question: have I forgiven my parents.

Yes, I have. It's not a hallmark card I-forgive-you-but-stay-away-from-me-forever type of forgiveness. It has been a completely transformative, unconditional love that the only explanation I have for it is that God healed me. For many years I harbored a great deal of resentment towards them. I felt like they were the reason that I had such a hard time at a young age. As I became a mother and grandmother I couldn't understand how you could treat a child so badly and expect them not to turn out the way that I did.

Please hear me when I say this: I don't believe that God causes people to mistreat and abuse their children. That's not what I'm saying at all. BUT, I do believe that He allows everything to take place for a specific reason. He knew that I would need a certain amount of internal toughness to be able to navigate my life to where I am now. I could not have ever survived my environment if I was soft or if I couldn't bring it when it needed to be brought.

I could bring it.

The Great Recovery

What I have learned today is that just because I wouldn't have chosen some of the things I went through to teach me how to become me, God, in His infinite wisdom knew exactly how to perfect the sculpture that is me today. He gave me the parents that I had, and today I love them very much. Every pain I had God used like an artist uses a tooth chisel, further eliminating rough valleys and peaks. In the end, which I haven't reached yet, I will be as smooth as porcelain and as strong as steel.

That is what I know.

Everything that the enemy tried to take from me God has given back to me 100 fold. I have a beautiful family of my own, wonderful grandchildren and more nieces and nephews than I can count. And while it hasn't always been easy some of the greatest joys in my life have been centered on them.

This book is not an end, but a new beginning of sorts. It's the opening of a new chapter that God has already written and has so graciously allowed me to live out. I don't know how the chapter ends, but I do know that it's designed for me and I'm designed for it. With that knowledge I know that I cannot lose.

In the bible in the book of Matthew, chapter 24 verse 13, it says "But he that shall endure unto the end, the same shall be saved." Whenever I watch a marathon race on television I think of this verse. Why? A marathon is 26.2 miles. At the beginning of the race hundreds of runners line up next to one another, all expecting to win. As the race progresses different packs of runners begin to form. The leaders typically run together while the vast majority stays way behind.

The thing about a marathon is that it tests not only the physical limitations of your body, but the emotional and psychological limits as well. How so? Medical science has proven that after about 13 miles the human body has used up most of its stored up fuels, like sugars and other carbohydrates. So, for the next 13.2 miles most runners are performing on sheer instinct and will power.

As the race progresses more and more runners start to fall off from the leaders pack for one reason or another. Now there are just a few runners leading the way. Over the next several miles the true leader of the pack eventually emerges. At the end of the race the better runners have what is known as a good "kick", which is a term used to describe how much sprinting ability they have left in their legs. Those runners who have a good "kick" usually finish strong and are heavy favorites to win.

As I enter into this next chapter of my life I feel like I still have the ability to "kick" strong. I look forward to the next field that God places me in. This time I know I'll consume it. Everything that I've gone through has been training for this race now. And you know what?

I don't plan on losing. I'm going to win. I've already won.

I'm the winner….and I look good while I'm doing it.

www.ingramcontent.com/pod-product-compliance
Lightning Source LLC
Chambersburg PA
CBHW070557100426
42744CB00006B/318